A QUAKER VOICE FOR PEACE

HATE

VIOLENCE

WAR

POEMS OF WITNESS AND PROTEST

HAROLD B. CONFER

Pleasant Word

Packaged by Pleasant Word, PO Box 428, Enumclaw, WA 98022. The views expressed or implied in this work do not necessarily reflect those of Pleasant Word. The author(s) is ultimately responsible for the design, content and editorial accuracy of this work.

ISBN 1-4141-0255-0
Library of Congress Catalog Card Number: 2004095897

Dedication

I dedicate this collection of poems to all of the peacemakers working for UN agencies and other NGOs trying to bring relief to the suffering in Iraq from our policies of starvation, bombs, and torture carried out on children, insurgents, citizens, all of them considered our enemies. Many peacemakers have died or been sorely wounded. Still others wait in Jordan for Americans to go home so they can once again attempt to relieve the suffering and return to Baghdad. See my poem "Target: Peacemakers.

Table of Contents

Special Thanks

When one has been a participant in poetry circles or other short-term intentional communities one learns to appreciate those who go out of their way to give positive feedback to speaking or writing. Since the publishing of *Finding My Voice* , I have been blessed with many who have written, e-mailed, or spoken to me about how my poems have spoken to their condition, as well as with suggestions to make them better. I thank you one and all. If you have a message you wish to share, leave it on my website, **<http//hjconfer.home.att.net>**

As in my previous writing, I am indebted to my wife June for her editorial as well as compassionate critical skills and support allowing time for this writing.

A Voice of Peace

This is a book of poetic satire and lament over a world at war in which God has been surgically removed from our lives by a violence worshiping government, by those of right wing fundamentalist Christian, Jewish and Moslem persuasions, and by our own cowardice to speak the truth of the gospel of love, forgiveness and trust.

I live in a city that was held hostage two years ago by a sniper and his associate, the leader trained by our military and obviously very good at his craft. This indiscriminate and willful violence, whether perpetrated by our President, a couple of snipers or being visited on us by Osama bin Laden has created a world which is a most real and immediate threat to us all. It hangs over us just as the threat of nuclear extinction hung over us during the Cold War. The reason the threat today is so real is that in the new millenium no one is safe anywhere. The reasons for this are clear. It was in this millenium that terrorists struck at our homeland but they did so in response to a long history of our country interfering in the affairs of others. At that point we had a very real choice: We could have pursued Osama bin Laden and brought him to trial in the World Court. Instead, we devastated Afghanistan in an unsuccessful attempt to capture him. Then, we invaded Iraq, our President lying about the existence of weapons of mass destruction and a link between Sadaam Hussein and bin Laden as the rationale for unilateral war. A year later, no weapons have been found and Rumsfeld himself admitted to the Congress there was no link between these two dictators. Most recently, the Senate Committee on Intelligence produced a report confirming most of the assertions made in this book causing members on both sides of the aisle to admit, had the truth been known, they most likely would not have voted to support the war. One member friendly to the President said candidly, had the President known the truth he could have pursued other options than war.

Like many others, I now find myself feelng personally guilty about the treatment of prisoners that were clearly abused, humiliated and killed in the name of the democracy we are forcing on Iraq. In a very real sense, we have created a world in which an Osama bin Laden was sure to come and will come again.

In my despair I wonder if the Democrats will come up with an agenda that is not just more of the same? Have we learned anything from two world wars, the Korean and Vietnam War and the present obliteration of Iraq?

I hope my poems speak about a real and scary world in which the innocent, peaceful and lovely growth of my grandchildren and all children is being threatened by a culture that proclaims the worship of violence as a simple solution to complex problems. Can we find hope in seeking truth and casting our lot for life?

Writing about peace in a time of devastating war is never easy. I weep daily for the young men and women (of both countries) put in harm's way and increasingly coming home in body bags which cannot be covered up by the Pentagon insisting we cannot view their silent flag-draped coffins arriving in Dover. The most recent exposure of truth, allowing the people to see it like it is, in Abu Ghraib prison, is one more legacy of a war conceived of in deceit, lied about its justifications, and claiming victory while the struggle and the destruction continue unabated.

The recent exodus of former Bush cabinet members and employees are testament to the American people of a most damning indictment of a President, at best asleep at the wheel and at worst so obsessed with Sadaam Hussein as to completely miss all the warning signs of the gathering storm that would result in the tragic events of 9/11. His inaction to possibly prevent that Al Qaeda attack is a clear dereliction of duty, an offence for which he should be impeached.

The President and the Pentagon have tried to not make the same mistakes as in Vietnam. This is to say they have attempted to put the media in bed (what a metaphor, embedded media, it reads like the best little whore house in Texas!) with our troops so that they will report their news from the Pentagon perspective.

But while we have lost hundreds, our overwhelming technology has killed thousands of Iraqis. It is also not lost on the surviving Iraqis that our food embargo before the hostilities began, killed hundreds of thousands of their children and at nutritional risk, poor and elderly.

Just these two facts alone are enough to explain why they hate us so, why our forced democracy will not be swallowed easily and other countries and contractors allied with us will also be treated as enemy targets. Did we learn nothing in Vietnam?

The Iraqis suffered under Sadaam Hussein and know oppression first hand. The fact that they cannot distinguish between his oppression and that of the US military led by George W. is nobody's fault other than ours.

The saddest thing to me is that we have stunning peacemakers alive and well whom George W. never once asked for advice. I suspect it is similar to the poets shunned by the White House two Valentine Days ago and the David Kays, Richard Clarkes and others who told George truths he did not want to hear.

My Quaker voice of peace reflects on those many stories of missed opportunities, messengers ignored and tragedy compounded by lies and deceit. We continue to travel down that road of violence, believing the ads by Haliburton, Lockheed and Northrup-Grumman that we have such technological superiority that we can completely dominate insignificant Iraq. It is an irony of history that these attitudes are remarkably similar to the attitudes of the British toward the American colonies during the time of our own Revolution.

I have no doubt that we can completely flatten Iraq, turning their country into a new Sahara desert. But this will be necessary to "win" which is just another word for "losing."

Rumsfeld recently made a hasty trip to Iraq and after a well televised series of pep rallies to bolster the flagging resolve of our soldiers, quietly opened the doors of Abu Ghraib and set half the captives free, many more to be released the next day. Damage control a little too late to save our image or any sense of innocence on the part of the chain of command which only stops with the commander in chief.

A scientist talking about the Chesapeake Bay being polluted by Pennsylvania farm land runoff said, "It's all based on a very sophisticated scientific principle: Water runs downhill." The chain of military command works like water, it runs downhill. The congress was correct to grill Rumsfeld and, while Rumsfeld was in Iraq, Paul Wolfowitz. The fact that Bush has publically supported Rumsfeld means he is just as guilty. Soldiers do not carry out atrocities unless they have direct orders or feel confident they will be supported by their commanders. Water runs downhill.

God help and forgive America and save what is left of Iraq from a violence—worshiping, imperialistic US.

As a Friend and as a builder I use plumblines to determine the straightness of a wall. As a Quaker poet and social critic, I use moral and ethical plumblines to judge the actions of others to better assess whether those actions follow their words. These unwavering values are a background to many of my poems. They are familiar to other Friends as they are the testimonies that bind us together and are the basis of all human community. You will find them throughout expressed as truth, equality, simplicity, and peace with justice.

I Want To Be

I want to be a poet
who reveres languages
and sings ballads, painting pictures of life
without popular obscenities
but still tells the truth.

I have been accused
of being very prejudiced
against George W. Bush
and for Jesus the Christ:
I stand guilty as charged.

Still, I want to honor
that of God within the breast of
even those that I find wanting.
I want them to demonstrate not just say
that God and the Prince of Peace
guide their life.

To tell the truth, George W. Bush
while President would much rather be king.
Perhaps this is why he and Tony
a comfortable duet sing.

George wants everyone
to fall on bended knee
to doff their cap, curtsey low,
proclaim their fealty.

No protestors here to object
or stand on conscience free,
"Bow down your heads
and keep quite still
except for praising me!"

He wants faith-based initiatives
using free tax dollars to bind up
the world's wounds. He hopes
if he can fill their pockets
they will not protest his tunes.

He makes sure, as only a king can do,
that through his unilateral war,
creating carnage and injustice too
he will keep his loyal knights busy
and exhaust the faith-based few.
Will King George ever listen
to the still small voice within?
I fear he's too busy making war
deafness caused by warring sin.

Is this why they always shout,
"Please God, save the king?"
Is this then the only hope
to end wars he can't win?

A bleak picture of King George,
I hope you all will see:
I have not used

one four-letter word,
not one obscenity!

To end this tragic ballad
and search for hope I say,
kingship's not hereditary here in USA

Presidential respect is earned
at home and abroad, every single day
walking a walk of truth and justice
right action being the only way.

It is my clear discernment—
as this president goes it alone
His sandy, oily, unilateral war
brought no credit to his throne.

I'll put my hope with peaceful others
as with humanity we sing
With no room for a prince of peace.
this man is not our king.

A Special Plea

"Deliver us from evil"
we pray it so quickly
it just rolls off our tongue
forgotten almost before it is said.

Yet it is the ultimate plea,
the climax of our Lord's prayer

Though we ask for bread
and ask for forgiveness
and ask not to be led
into temptation
the real whammy
is when we ask to be
delivered from evil.

I'm sorry, Lord, but it seems,
as I read the daily news,
as if a lot of evil seems
to be avoiding your
clutches.

Is that because we do not pray
earnestly or sincerely enough
or because delivery from evil
was a bigger task than even
Jesus thought when he taught
us thus to pray?

Lord, you know I could do with
a little hunger, and I pretty
regularly ask for forgiveness
and try to forgive others.
And knowing my own sins
I try to avoid temptation
but I cannot easily deal
with evil.

So this is the plea that I
utter over and over;
my Quaker litany,
"deliver us from evil,

Lord, are you listening?

Ferlinghetti, you were wrong!

To say that no one speaks
is to ignore the thousands who demonstrated in
cities all over this earth.

To say that no one speaks
is to ignore the signs in my front yard and many others
bumper stickers on many cars
"War is not the answer."

To say that no one speaks
is to ignore the preachers in main-line churches,
shouting from the pulpit to the people,
"It's the oil, God's people,
that's why we are there!"

To say that no one speaks
is to ignore the prestigious parliamentarians, select
scientists and able academics from many countries
who attempted to point out
American stockpiles of

weapons of mass destruction
yesterday in Aberdeen.

To say that no one speaks
is to ignore the media's unwillingness
to give equal time to the forces of peace
and justice but always
slobbering to interview
Powell or Bush.

It's a brilliant poem, Larry
but it doesn't tell the truth.
Never has there been a more united, world-wide,
articulate opposition to a war than we have today.
The problem, Ferlinghetti, my friend,
is one of choices.
Bush chooses not to listen.
Laura chooses not to hear
anti-war poetry and cancels
the White House poetry reading.

Powell and the Pentagon are not
subject to the popular will.

The media muted for fear they will be
become personna non grata
in the corridors of power.
But again, this is a
choice the media
mogels made.

Choices made to target all Arabs
for the sins of a few.
Choices made to strip away our
personal liberties because of
what you rightly expose as
a "vast paranoia."

I suspect, if we survive this
next few months that many Americans
will take their voting rights much more seriously
and demand that the candidate that gets
the popular vote must necessarily
assume power.

Not just a powerful political oil family
able to manipulate the election
because too many made the
choice not to protest at
that point.

At that critical divide you may
have been correct—
Not enough spoke their truth to
avoid a future catastrophe.

Letter to Bayard Rustin

I'm sorry we never met
though we marched on a parallel path.

As you were preparing to assist
King in Montgomery, June was already
finding disfavor at the University of Chattanooga
while I was savoring international workcamping.

While you strategized with King to plan
the great March on Washington we were going
to work for Julius Nyerere in (then) Tanganyika.

I am glad you had a Quaker mother
and you felt a part of her spiritual tradition.
I am glad you went to India to steep yourself
in the Gandhian philosophy of satyigraha.

I am especially glad you were able to teach King
about *Ahimsa* so that he could integrate
satyigraha with his own powerful Christianity.

But what many do not know is how you
were able to negotiate with the Metro
police and even the New York police
to work in and around the great march
unarmed,

No flashpoints as no one was bearing arms
or arming bears. A legacy that is still needed
as we still attempt to influence those
who control the world economy.

I was proud to serve as the last civil rights lobbyist for the FCNL
though you should have applied. But by this time
you were seeing the reality of world hunger
and unjust economic structures,
as you learned about
politics from LBJ,
your mentor.

You failed us on Vietnam; while you could have led.
I expect if you had listened to your mama more
and LBJ less, you could have played a vital
leadership role to try to bring the war
to a speedy end.

And now, dear friend, we need you even more
and what articulate black Quaker is going
to take your place?

In many ways you were before your time
but thanks to you, the legacy is there.
You not only helped break the back
of white supremacy but you
raised the gay issue
and got crucified.

But someone had to walk this path
though we still have miles to go
Homophobia is alive and well
in the black community
as well as in the white

But slowly we are learning that others
we thought were so strange are
just like me.

The love of your Quaker mama will still
overcome. We will one day find
that dream of one human
family with much diversity
to be an achievable
goal.

So rest well, dear Friend. We are
eagerly awaiting the next
charismatic Friend to
walk your walk
in new shoes.

Lord, Let Me Be an Instrument of thy Peace

Lord, let me be,
let me be an instrument,
apparatus, appliance, contraption,
device, gadget, means,
utensil, tool, vessel
of thy peace.

Lord, let me be
let me be, be, being,
is, now, here, here and now
fill my being and let me be thine
Serve you by singing your song
having the courage to be
your instrument in this
sour-filled world.

Simplicity 101
All People Have Needs

Education should teach us about ourselves, our needs,
and how to satisfy those needs while living
in community on an earth with limited
resources. It is also about
understanding others
have needs not
dissimilar to ours.

The need for clean air—the breath of all life.
The need for clean water—the basis of good health
and good agriculture.
The need for personal security—so families in community
can grow and thrive in peace.
The need for food—tonight, millions will go to bed
hungry or malnourished.
This need not be.
The need for education—to give all children
chances and choices and real world skills.
The need for freedom—to make choices real
The need for justice—to make sure that bounty
and opportunity are shared by all.

The need for good housing—to ensure good health
and security.
The need for health care—provided on the basis of need
not by the ability to pay.
The need for old-age security—so all elders can
face death with dignity.

Now, if we understand our needs
and those of others we need to
learn how to compromise
so the needs of all
can be met with
fairness to all.

Simplicity 102
Improving our Understanding and Compromises

So, we have chosen peace.
We have decided to be peacemakers.
We know that we have needs and others do too.
We are willing to compromise so that
we can live together in peace.

But part of learning to live together
is to distinguish between needs and wants.
The earth just cannot support
conspicuous consumption.

To share equitably we need to ensure
that everyone's needs are being met.

This requires us to take a hard look
at those things we buy and ask
"Will this new thing
better meet my needs?
Or is it something
I don't need to have
or something I can
share with others?"

Simple questions for us all
but essential in our
search for peace.
Living simply
so others may
simply live.

Eco Poetry
Living Downstream

Caring for the earth and Her people
as we are part of the same village
like it or not.

We all live
downstream, desperately
trying to clean our own water
enough to drink and air to breathe
while sending our waste on downstream as
the other's problem. As the poisons people put
in the water and air float downstream they are carried
by wind and rain. Can we not see no one is any longer
safe? We are all living downstream, one from another.
Everyone is down stream to someone else, and we are
growing people so fast even our best attempts to clean our
water and air and care for those who live downstream as well
as ourselves seems poor at best. India a case in point with
16% of the world's people but 2% of the land and only 4%
of the water, its 1 billion people will swell to 1½ billion in
a mere 25 years. How much cataclysm will it take before
we rescue all that energy and wealth we now put into
making war and invest it into survival, not just
of starving people but of creating lives of
quality, worth living for us all? Who
lives down stream to you?
Where do you dump
your garbage?

Mark Yourself For Truth

In this crazy world bent on war
truth is the first casualty
So in desperation
I turn to truthful
duct tape.

I cut off a strip about 12" long
and write on it in big letters
with black magic marker

"Protection from Weapons
of Mass Destruction"

If I have space at the end of
the strip I draw a frowning
smiley face.
☹
I now wear this duct tape
protection as an
armband.

And another where a name tag
should grace my jacket.

Since the truth that we are all
part of one human family
and family members
do not kill each other
has been lost

Friends, let us wear this as a protest
for all to see and join us to say
that we are all laughing
at our politicians
and President
and hope
they have their
own duct tape handy
so when the weapons
fly, they will be protected
just like their silly followers.

Truth: the First, Middle and Last Casualty.

When we speak of truth as being the first casualty of war,
we ignore the fact that truth will continue to be burned
as a sacrificial offering to the god of war
and everyone will emulate the
leaders who lie to obscure
the truth.

Bush lies to say why we had to go to war.
Rumsfeld lies about not knowing
about inhumane treatment in
Abu Ghraib.

Ashcroft lies about similar treatment of detainees
in Guantanamo.

Halliburton lies about the price of petrol
to gouge the Pentagon and us.

Our soldiers were ordered through the chain of command
to humiliate and abuse prisoners to gather
military intelligence, an oxymoron,
from Abu Ghraib to Guantanamo

and in many other prisons
in between.

Now everyone in this chain of command,
from the soldier's immediate supervisors
all the way up to President Bush
are lying about those orders
so the soldiers can
take the fall.

The soldiers will now be the new burnt offering
lying in the ashes of truth on the sacrificial
altar of the god of war.
which is the god
we worship.

Hail Mars!

Are You There, George?

Are you there, George? Playing "God"
by acting as if you are God Herself?
How do you have the audacity
to threaten the life of mankind
while clearly not having the
capacity to think this through?

You've destroyed our economy, most peoples savings' lost.
Now pouring plowshares into swords
you seek bloody war.

Stupid man! War is a game where no one wins.
You may think that unilateral war makes
you a fine, bold leader.

But the other side of that coin reads:
arrogant,
foolhardy,
insolent,
cavalier
and haughty.

Not the capacities we look for
nor desire in a president.

But link those repugnant attitudes
with the power to cause a rain of
death and destruction as the
world has never seen and
George, you scare me!

It's not just what you have done
in Afghanistan but
what you do in Iraq.

The world in a shambles before you go
playing God, pushing all others aside.
Learning well from Sadaam Hussein
how to a political bully be.

God is going to have a pretty big heart
to include US as a part of Her
human family when you are through,
But it's not just what you are doing to us
but what you may do to the world
in the process of your perfidity.
Not just a betrayal of trust
in your oath of office
but your betrayal
of the tenuous
strings that
hold us all
together as
one family
under God.

Playing God is a dangerous game,
George. Like war, it's another
of those games you can't
win but as you play,
we can all lose.

Osama bin Laden,
You and George have the
same dreadful disease: you
playing Allah, George, playing God.
Now your attack on the twin towers
has delivered us into the hands of King
George who might pursue you but more
likely will pursue Sadaam Hussein
and may well bring us all down
in the pursuit.

Thanks Be to Thee

I suspect, as God looks down
on her fragile earth today, She might
likely say,..

"Thank you, friends—
all you who demonstrated in over
600 cities all over the earth to witness
for peace on earth.

Thank you, friends—
all those who went to Iraq
to identify and destroy their
weapons of mass destruction.

Thank you, friends—
all those who went to Aberdeen
to try to expose the world's
largest stockpile of
such weapons.

Thank you, friends—
all you who carry signs,
put them in your yard,
stick them on your car
to witness for peace
on earth.

Thank you, friends—
for writing, calling,
faxing your leaders
to witness for peace
on earth.

Thank you, friends—
those who are willing
to go to jail and suffer
for your witness for peace
on earth.

Thank you, friends—
for praying to me
and hoping I will intervene
to stop this madness. But you
need to know, dear friends,
that it is out of my hands.
I gave you, in eager expectation,
the freedom to make choices.
You have made choices
to put power in the hands
of those who choose
war over peace.

Now those who live by the sword
will die by the sword
and sadly take many
innocent others
with them.

I have tried to speak to these
in power through the words
of others for many years.
I even sent my son
to make my will
as clear as
possible.

But you keep making choices
trusting violence over love.
in spite of my prophets,
dreamers, poets,
and too many
others to count.

It's a make or break situation
in our world today and only you
have the power to stop the
madness. I gave you
that power to bring
peace on earth.

So, dear friends,
don't blow it!
What more can I do?
I'm only God."

Don't Even Go There

A prediction of sad decision making

Said so much more gently by Robert Frost,
today's generation seems to require less poetic
and much more direct wisdom.

But the same wisdom applies.
Present choices determine future choices
and that makes all the difference.

When Nixon was attempting to double
the capacity of federal prisons because
he did not have enough room to lock up
Vietnam war protesters, we realized
the political truth in building prisons:
"If you build them
they cannot stand empty."
You must fill them, no matter how very
successful pre-trial diversion or
rehabilitation.
If you build them
they cannot stand empty.

Today we are faced with another president
determined to go to war.
He has recommended, then
rejected UN inspections;
he has recommended, then
rejected a second UN resolution;
he has recommended, then
rejected Sadaam's willingness
to destroy Iraqi missiles.

Instead, he has steadily surrounded Iraq
with over 200,000 soldiers and a
frightening array of munitions
all trained on Iraq.

The political truth of preparing for war is similar
to the truth in building prisons:
It is political suicide to spend money
building up for a war that is then averted.

Would that Daddy Bush could have
taught George the lesson,
"Don't even go there."

Because once you get there, all the generals
will ask, "Well?' The prevention of war
now no longer an option.
Now the question
is "when?"

I suspect that if Sadaam disarmed
tomorrow it would not be enough.
to stop this war.

George is going to have his war
as he has already gone there.
The political truth is
if you build them
they cannot stand empty.

Likewise, if you go toward war,
already spending one million
dollars every minute,
politically you will be required
to go into war.

This is why we try to teach our children
about the importance of making choices
Because once you build them
they cannot stand empty.

It will take a bigger man than
Nixon or Bush to admit
they were wrong so
what about claiming victory
and allowing the UN
to disarm Iraq?

We can look over their shoulder
but it is still time to stand down.
in peace.

Smart vs. Dumb

After six months of agony; a girl-child abducted.
The challenger lost. The hawks gearing up for war
while the people of the world
are protesting for peace
in cities everywhere.

She who was lost has been found.
The family and friends and
community and nation exalt.
Praise God!

It is smart to give praise to a merciful God
who protected Elizabeth Smart.

But dumb to continue to prepare
to obliterate other little girls
who will be found
by our bombs.

A precious Smart child found while
other precious lives targeted
by our smart bombs.
Having gifted us,
how can this same God
forgive our warring madness?

I Don't Plant Trees Anymore

When I was a young man I wanted to help change the world.
I first aimed for the Methodist ministry. Then I honored
an earlier leading and became a conscientious objector
and discovered the Society of Friends.

Two years of alternative service turned into seven years
service in Africa mixed with a stunning year at Pendle Hill
We joined the Quakers, for better or for worse,
while in Providence, Rhode Island.

Moving to DC and serving the FCNL we also bought some land
next to some friends and I started planting trees.
It has been said, it takes an optimist
to plant trees. That was me.

Now, the divorce of our neighbors, a brain tumor,
a serious car accident and a fall from a ladder later,
we sold the land with its beautiful trees.
I don't plant trees anymore.

But still out to change the world I found my voice as a poet.
As most poets, I write on a variety of things

but as a Friend I also write poems
in support of the peace testimony
of my small worshiping community.

When I first published a book of poems warning
of an impending war in Iraq, warning of
relying on violence to solve human problems,
I offered to read some to the
residents of Friends House,
a "Quaker" elders home.

A Friend took the suggestion to the program committee,
herself a published poet and one of my mentors.
She returned the slim volume with the word
that the committee said "no" as the poems
were too controversial; too anti-Bush.

To say I wasn't wounded would be to lie.
But now that we are gripped in a
horrendous war and Bush
propelled us down this path
I want to say, "I told you so."
Quakers are a small part of our population
Quaker poets even more so. We are not
under any illusion about our power to
change the world but I was heartened
when Laura Bush canceled
a poetry reading on
Valentine's Day
because
the poets had
decided to read
anti-war poems to
protest the impending war
and her husband's policies of
death and destruction in the world.

In good company with Mark Twain
who in the face of patriotic fever
as we fought to subdue the

Filipinos tried to get his
"War Prayer" published
to no avail.

So it is a little bit of consolation to know that
I am in good company with even our
own national poet laureate being
denied his voice but it is still sad
that censorship is alive and well
from the White House
to Friends House.

We live far enough from Iraq that we do not hear
the sounds of the bombs and screams of
the dying at our hands.

Instead, we use ear plugs
so we don't have to hear those
who protest the creation of such a world.
It's disturbing to be told that we put him in office
and we will pay for this war

I met Chuck from Friends House yesterday at Kaiser
we were, both of us, old men getting new glasses
Me because of three bouts of laser surgery
Chuck because he flunked his driver's exam.
Will our new eyes allow us to see
the world as it really is?

I don't know about Chuck.
As for me,
I don't plant trees anymore,
but I still try to write
peace poetry.

Killing Hussein and His Sons

Last night, so important as to interrupt
the final game of NCAA basketball tournament,
it was cautiously announced we may have
killed Sadaam Hussein, his two sons
and some other high-level
Iraqi military persons.

Military intelligence (an oxymoron)
was admittedly not as good as that
which informed our pre-emptive
bomb dropped on them before
we started the war.
(72 hours before schedule)
but it was too good to pass up
a "target of opportunity."

Of course we killed at least 10
civilians and injured scores of others
but that has been the pattern all war long.
Collateral damage running 20 to 1.
A major difference
from past wars.

Unfortunately, we have no DNA
from Hussein or his immediate family
so we will never know for certain
if we got this rogue or not.

Why do I not feel any pride in this mission?
Why do I mourn for the innocents
killed and injured with impunity?
Why did we spend the millions
to send this one B-52 with its
expensive load of death
over this residential
area of Baghdad?

If we knew where he was and if, as we have been told,
we "own" Baghdad, then why not send those
vaunted and much less expensive
special operations soldiers in to take him out?
I know the answer, teacher!
I suspect we do not own Baghdad and
that we have been lied to, once again.

But more important than lying, we have
enormous wealth so, why not spend it?
Since the Pentagon and the President
care not one whit for innocent
civilians slaughtered, this
is why we sent in
our shiny B-52
and its four expensive
bunker-buster bombs
The taxpayers will pay for it
plus we can save our soldiers' lives
for less hazardous duty. in Mosul.

But, what if they didn't get him?
Will we then weep for the
innocents killed?

Why start now?

Winning the War by Decapitating a Statue

Our people are euphoric!
We have entered Baghdad and
decapitated a statue of Sadaam.
Parents of the two grinning marines
interviewed, bursting with pride.

It is clear we are winning the war.
We have counted our dead—
just over a hundred,
a modest price
to pay for oil.

The media does not keep running
figures of the number we killed
by "friendly fire." (Some friends)
Has anyone bothered to count
the number of Iraqi solders
killed or missing?
Can anyone begin to count
the number of Iraqi
civilians killed or
buried alive by

our bunker—
busting bombs?

Who cares anyway?

We went to kill Sadaam Hussein. While there is still
no evidence we accomplished this.
we did, however, decapitate
a statue or two.

We went to expose the UN weapons inspectors
were not doing their jobs. So far, we have
not found any weapons of mass destruction.
Perhaps they were doing their jobs.
after all.

We went to liberate a country and to have access to its oil
We won, they lost. It's simple, stupid.
But what will this adventure cost?
Not just in money but in
civil liberties, loss of
allies, freedom at
home, loss of
credibility
in the world?

Iraq has lost an infrastructure
Now the 5,000,000 people in
Baghdad have less than
before we "gave" them
freedom.

The American Empire is alive and well.
We are winning the war
We can thumb our nose
at the rest of the world.

We can continue to guzzle gas
and consume goods we don't need.
We have new markets for our food and

other, less useful products in Iraq.
They can pay us in oil.

We will cheer home the troops
while Iraq still buries their dead.

Bush does not want the UN
to be involved in a post war Iraq
At least not until B & B
have divided the spoils.
Such is the nature of war.
Always has been,
always will be.

Let's hear it for our superb technology—
enabling us to kill without having
to hear their screams, see their
wounds, or count their dead.

Now we can decapitate a statue
to claim victory, adopt a few
Iraqi orphans and feel good
about our magnanimity.

Songs for an American Empire: The (New) Star Spangled Banner

1.
Oh, say can you see, by the bright green night light
with night technology we can kill them while they can't see.
And won't it be fair, with bombs bursting in air,
by killing them blind, they will never see their plight.
We now own the night
as well as the day
we can kill and rejoice
as we blow them away—
Oh God, we do thank thee for giving us this easy victory,
we can kill them all night long, and never hear their song!

2.
Oh, say can you hear, our good patriots cheer
as we turn your towns to tombs, we kill you to make you free.
And won't it be neat, to kill you in your sleep.
with bomb after bomb, we can kill without a qualm.
We now own the night
as well as the day
we can kill and rejoice
as we blow them away—

Oh God, we do thank thee for giving us this easy victory,
By killing without ears we don't need to hear their tears.

3.

Oh say can you see, by the light of our bombs
the rubble that we leave as we strive to make them free
They weep and they moan, as we hit them at home
we can bomb them in bed or starve them out instead.
We now own the night
as well as the day
we can kill and rejoice
as we blow them away—
Oh God, we do thank thee for giving us this easy victory,
By killing without eyes, we don't need to see their cries.

4

Oh, say can you feel, this terrible ordeal,
As you huddle in your homes our bombs will crush your bones
With no water or food we will teach you to feud;
before human rights you must learn that might makes right!
We now own the night
as well as the day
we can kill and rejoice
as we blow them away—
Oh God, we do thank thee for giving us this easy victory
By killing from afar, we need never see their scars

Songs for an American Empire: An de Crumbs be fallin' all aroun'

To the tune of "Joshua fit de battle of Jericho"
in the playful remembrance of Jester Hairston

Chorus
Halliburton got der hans in de cookie jar,
de cookie jar, de cookie jar,
Halliburton got der hans in de cookie jar,
an de crumbs be fallin, all aroun.'

1
We say dis is a fine company
led by our VP Dick Cheney
But all we see is de cookie jar
an de crumbs be fallin' all aroun.'

2
Halliburton sey de give Iraqi's some gas
But I tink dey done kicked us in de ass
De charged us for de hi-test fuel,
with regular runnin' all aroun.'

3
De company sey is de man's mistake
he got his han in de cookie jar
but dis in de way we fight our wars
Wi de crumbs a fallin' all aroun.'

4
Oh big fat profit is de name of de game,
Halliburton say it was a silly shame
Now dey is busy wid TV ads,
but de crumbs be fallin all aroun.'

5
While our naive troops fight and toil
Bush and crew have der hans on de oil
dat Democracy only be a big foil
Wi de crumbs a fallin all aroun.'

6
Dis smushed in President, he go to war
while de voters are left so very sore
Halliburton is serving de people now,
Wi' de crumbs a fallin' all aroun.'

Songs for an American Empire: A Patriotic Song for the Superbowl

"Oh say can you see, by the dawn's early light,
if there are weapons in Iraq, we will find them to our delight."
So sang David Kay, a hard looking,
optimistic UN weapons inspector.

"Oh we looked and we looked, from dawn to twilight,
but try as we might, we found no weapons in sight."
So reported David Kay to the UN
and to the world.

"We looked in the hills,
and in cities too,
we even more than once
looked in Hussein's swimming pool.
We never, no never in spite of all our valiant effort,
did see a single one, weapon of mass destruction!"
A good song, sung
by an honest man.

After Bush ignored the message and invaded Iraq anyway,
a not-so-secret ambition, he decided to rehire
the messenger, Kay, as he was an honest man.

Certainly, with the resources of the CIA,
all of our hovering satellites and other
boastful intelligence technology.
1,000 special forces
interviewing Iraqi
scientists, an
unlimited budget,
and no restrictions as to
where they could inspect
he would sing a different tune..

So, David Kay came home,
cleared his throat and sang
if in a slightly different key,
new words to the old tune:

"Oh say we did see, as we looked night and day
in his palaces of gold, and countless warehouse holes.
We had mighty lenses in our satellites too,
we could count the fleas in Sadaam Hussein's zoo.
We looked without hindrance
all over his state
But all we have to show,
is one still empty plate!
In spite of our efforts and spending all your money,
we bring the same old message; there ain't no weapons, honey!"

This unwelcome message if to a popular tune
will not be sung at the superbowl soon.

Instead we will gather
to play our national game
and watch dear Janet in her
Victorian secret bra, shed her shirt,
done without any shame—
to help us in this time of trauma
to momentarily forget the truth
of David Kay, the same
who implied so clearly,
(he being an honest man)

that King George chose to lie so vile,
just to make his daddy smile
and invade Iraq all the while..

With bombs bursting in air,
and our flag still there . . .
Ignoring the truth that
David Kay did share.

We will proudly weep for patriots lost
and refuse to see they died for naught.

Paying for War

The Iraq war is and will
cost us through the nose.
And you and I and our children
and grandchildren will pay for this.

Fiscal conservative Bush
has now run up an unbelievable
deficit. It will take generations of cost
cutting domestically and higher taxes to
pay for our brilliant war technology.

Not only did we have to build it
in the first place, but then we had to
feed the voracious god of war with bombs,
shells, missles, bullets, grenades, rockets,
and fuel, don't forget the oil or the food
all of which we used as if they were free.

Then we have to replace
all of the war machines we lost
either to friendly or unfriendly fire.
The "defense" industry licking their chops.

Billions and billions we pay for past,
present, and future wars—paid by you
and me in a myriad of ways: Taxes, of course,
with a massive percentage to pay for past war debts,
present war expenditures and then the constant cost of
developing new weapons systems to keep ahead of the pack.

But we also pay by having to defer
what we should be spending on education
and health care, services for the elderly and to
protect what environment we have left. The quality
of our air and water is decreasing because we are not looking
for solutions to these problems which may serve to be much
more difficult that removing the Republican Guard in Iraq.

Clearly we have some legitimate battles to fight.
Unfortunately, we are fighting the wrong battles and
we will pay dearly for those battles we are fighting and
for the ones we must fight or not survive.

The massive deficit we have developed in war
(because we can't pay for everything now) will not
just be paid by us but by our children and grand children.
They will carry this giant burden of war debt and pay it down
little by little, year after year.

Our children will also carry the burden
of there not being any new money for schools
or hospitals, roads or sewers, water development
or protection. Defer your dreams for inner or outer space.

We must pay for wars and they are always
much more expensive that the generals or the
President are willing to admit. But patriots are like sheep.
They are as eagerly infected by war fever as by Mad Cow Disease.
Patriot leaders fall into step behind the President. So the Congress
becomes a vital part of the war machine.

But we, not the Congress, will pay
for this war, past wars, and future wars.
We will pay and get our kids and grandkids
to pay because in the long run it is cheaper than
having to admit that war was not and is not the answer.

So far we have ignored the human cost—
the lives of our young men and women lost
or permanently disabled. Our patriots rush to fill
our hearts with praise for their "necessary" sacrifice.
But no amount of propaganda can gloss over the void
as we struggle to justify their use as cannon fodder by our
leaders feeding the voracious war machine.

What of the cost to Iraq? A whole generation
lost. Their infrastructure destroyed. We rush to
repair the airport while looting adds to the cost of recovery.
Given our history of assistance to Afghanistan I would not wait
for food from America. We starved their children before the war
and they are still starving now. But here's the logic:

We attacked them because they were such a threat.
Therefore, they deserved the cost of this war and
they must and will bear the cost of recovery.
They can and will
pay us in oil.
Or else.

The 10 Commandments of Occupation by the American Empire

Based on Exodus 20:1–17

1. Thou shalt not have any other gods other than Mars, the god of war.

2. Thou shalt not make a graven image except for those of George Bush, Tony Blair, and our god, Mars.

3. Thou shalt not take the name of God in vain unless provoked by coalition enemies or anti-war demonstrators.

4. Remember the Sabbath and keep it Holy except when called upon to make war. Then you may kill on any day necessary as the god of war is a demanding god.

5. Honor your father and mother unless they are pacifists and oppose this war.

6. You shall not murder except for the glory of Queen and Country.

7. You shall not commit adultery unless asked by your superiors to do so for your country.

8. You shall not steal except Iraqi oil or any other spoils of war. Remember, to the victor go the spoils!

9. You shall not bear false witness against your neighbor unless he is in Iraqi prisons. Then you can abuse and humiliate him as instructed.

10. You shall not covet your neighbor's house, wife, servants or possessions unless he is Iraqi or of Iraqi descent. Then, enjoy, enjoy!

The Bush and Blair Beatitudes

Based on Matthew 5:1–11

1. Blessed are those who are poor in spirit for they shall be allowed to loot to their hearts content.

2. Blessed are those who mourn for we shall make sure there are plenty of dead.

3. Blessed are the meek for we shall steal their oil to pay for our devastation.

4. Blessed are those who hunger and thirst for truth as we will condition their perception of truth by putting them in bed with our troops.

5. Blessed are the merciless. We shall kill Sadaam Hussein, his sons, other family, Republican Guard, regular Army, and Islamic insurgents as opportunities are presented in Guantanamo and Abu Ghraib prison without mercy.

6. Blessed are the impure in heart as we shall give them full reign, under the Patriot Act, to violate any Iraqi's human rights

7. Blessed are the warmakers for they shall be called patriots.

8. Blessed are those who are persecuted and if you oppose this war we shall make sure you will be persecuted, beyond the fullest extent of the Patriot Act.

9. Blessed are you when you support this wonderful war and say all manner of evil against those who oppose our glorious war, calling them cowards and traitors.

10. Rejoice and be exceeding glad for great will be our reward as we carve up Iraq into the spoils of war.

The Great Commandment

Thou shalt love the god of war and your neighbor's oil as you do your own.

Bonding Around a Defining Moment

This Good Friday I am led to thoughts of goodness and hope.
Along with the families and friends of the rescued seven
prisoners of war in Iraq,
I rejoice in their rescue and recovery.
Anytime you can minimize the suffering caused in war
it is a good thing.
Of course, if we had not gone to war in the first place,
we could have avoided a lot more suffering.
Still I rejoice when people whose lives are threatened are rescued
and they can celebrate with their family a whole new
meaning to the word "resurrection."

At the same time I weep for Iraqi humanitarians we have imprisoned
because they attempted to send food and medicine to alleviate
starvation in their country of origin.

This morning a military spokesperson talked of the bonding
that has occurred among these seven soldiers.
He said, "They will be friends for life.
They share a defining moment in their lives."
Friends, we don't need war or the military
to produce bonding around a common mission.

In the church rebuilding workcamps
that became a major domestic response
to the arson attacks on houses of worship in the 1990's,
we had a couple thousand volunteers
who came to rebuilding sites and for a week at a time
helped rebuild arson-burned churches.
They all realized, in retrospect,
that this was also a defining moment in their lives.
They too bonded with their fellow volunteers of amazing diversity.
Protestants, Catholics, Jews, Moslems, and the unchurched
lived and worked together in peace.
To a person they reported at the end that they had
been given so much more
by the church members, that community, and the other volunteers
than they had been able to give. In light of the reality that the
accumulated effort of these volunteers has seen
eight different burned churches
rebuilt, no small feat.

Highlights to the bonding occurred in a variety of
situations, but I remember
when a young student cantor sang the Song of Lamentations
on the burn site of Mount Zion Baptist Church as part of
the Jewish fast day of *Tish B'av.*[†]
While we all shared in this very moving interfaith prayer service,
the heavens opened and it poured God's tears on this site
of devastation caused by racial hatred.
Later, this young cantor, Michael Mandel, would write in
our book of reflections
his insights of his week in Alabama of sacred work as a
Jew rebuilding
a burned Baptist Church. He noted in closing that when the rains
came down during the service, he was led to witness,
"The rains of redemption will always
extinguish the fires of humanity.

† Tish B'av is a yearly holy day for fasting to remember the burning of the Temple of Jerusalem. Our Jewish volunteers always lead our worship on this day.

Such is my faith."
This became one of the defining moments
for all the diverse volunteers, staff,
and church members who shared in that remarkable week.
Their bonding and realization of their meaningful role
in a peaceful solution to a violent disaster
was expressed most eloquently
by the Rabbi advisor to this small
group of rabbinical students,
Nancy Weiner, when she wrote,
"If when Hitler burned many synagogues
on Krystalnacht in Germany, there had been
such an outpouring of volunteers to help
rebuild as has happened this summer
in Green County, Alabama, World
War II would have never occurred."

Is it just possible that these two thousand angels of peace
who flew to rebuilding sites in Alabama, Mississippi,
South and North Carolina,
Texas and Maryland helped to prevent a race war in America as it
said to the forces of evil, "we will not tolerate this arson. Burn
down these churches and we shall rebuild them!"
One of the visiting African American pastors from a northern
church wrote,
"If the first arsonist that burned the first church in 1995
could have seen what a glorious response of angels
of peace his arson would cause he would have
never lit that match."
Bonding around defining moments is one of the fruits
of human united action.
But it has transformative power when exercised working as God's
hands and feet; as peace makers and builders
in Her world as a conscious part of Her diverse family.
We don't need the military to teach us
about "defining moments."

Make Love, Not War

A slogan of the Vietnam era—
still a valuable imperative.

Making peace is hard work
easier to say than to do.
It is extremely difficult after
war has become a reality

We have discovered much
about those who profit off of war.
Not just the builders of weapons
but also those awaiting anarchy.

They loot the buildings of the
rich but also steal the invaluable
artifiacts from the national museum.

Iraq and Iran, the cradles of
ancient civilization, have seen
much senseless destruction.

When Alexander the Great
marched through these lands with
his war elephants, he destroyed
the early library of the Parsee
civilization containing poetry
and scriptures of rare beauty.

That library lost forever,
civilization has never recovered
from that devastation. What
assurance do we have that
"modern" war using bunker
busting bombs will not commit
any lesser atrocities?

It seems there was an organized
crime gang just awaiting the
anarchy that occurred in Baghdad
following our shock and awe
preemptive bullying.
War is so predictable!
They had bribed locals so had
access through keys and security
codes. They methodically stole
while the coalition forces were
busy making war against a
desperate and poor people
and ironically running
interference for the thieves.

A people rich in heritage
now we have facilitated
criminals stealing or destroying
this history as well.

Bush's gain is the world's loss.
Not any different from past wars
except we can kill more quickly

from a greater distance and we
don't leave any elephant dung.

Alexander's elephants or
Bush's tanks wasting precious
lives and antiquities three
thousand years apart.

When will we learn to
make love, not war?
Have we learned nothing
in those intervening
three thousand years?

Easter in Baghdad 2003

"Dateline Baghdad.
Just after midnight, a wounded man
was seen to be emerging from
a pile of stone rubble, shaking the
dust from off his shroud.

He walked toward a hospital
picking up a wounded child from
off the street. When he arrived, he
gave the child to an overworked nurse.

He walked from bed to bed
reassuring those who were terrified,
soothing pain, making children smile.

He helped hold the hand of a scared
woman giving birth by the light of
a kerosene lamp; he uttered words
of encouragement to the nurses
and a lone doctor who couldn't
remember when last
they slept.

As he prepared to leave,
he went by the morgue where
hundreds of distraught Iraqi people
were searching for lost loved ones.

He uttered a soft prayer in Arabic
as he comforted each person in line
the tears running down his shroud.
He was seen walking into the dawn
his face an agony of grief.

American and British snipers held him
in their cross hairs just in case
he was a suicide bomber.

One over eager lad pulled his trigger
and the figure disappeared.
"Who was that?" asked
the Sergeant.
"I'm sure it was a terrorist; he was
wearing a turban," exclaimed
the proud Marine.
The platoon deployed
to find the body.

But all they ever found was a tall
male Arab with what looked like
fresh wounds in his hands and feet
and a gaping hole in his side.

"Looks like you got him, Joseph,"
commended the Sergeant.
But Joseph had a haunted
look when he saw that the
wound in his side where he had
shot the man had no exit wound.

As the soldiers went back to their
posts the Sergeant again
commended their vigilance.

"You men keep up the
good work and we
will all be home by
Christmas!"

As the man lay by the side of the road
small streams of water and blood
flowed from his wounds and
the tears ran down his face
and that of the marine.

The sun broke, blood red over the horizon.
Village women carried his body
to a shallow grave and covered
him with stones."

"This is David Bloom reporting on
early Easter morning from a
rock cairn in Baghdad."

Greetings and Salutations

Hail George, American Emperor,
pursuer of Sadaam and other terrible tyrants.
The creator of the infamous deck of cards
with people pictured already convicted as guilty
without the waste of trial by jury.

We praise thy sovereign nose that can sniff out
weapons of mass destruction
better than on-site UN inspectors
but cannot smell those as close as Aberdeen.

We stand in awe of your ability to destroy a country to kill one man.
We are blessed to have a caring president who will rebuild Iraq
using their oil to pay for its reconstruction.

We will serve you, your willing soldiers, as we never
question authority.
We believe everything you say because you have been born again.
We have been trained to live by the motto,
"Our commander, right or wrong!"

To your glory you have taught us other ancient wisdom such as,
"Might makes right," and "To the victor go the spoils.."

We worship your "shock and awe" technology
assuring us we can kill many of the enemy from very far away
so we don't have to hear their screams or see their agony.

We sing songs of praise for superior optics
so we can obliterate their people at night while they
can't even see us.

Thank you for thumbing your proud nose at allies,
domestic demonstrators, and world opinion
as this makes us feel superior.

Thank you for making sure our media are in bed with our troops
so they can see the war from your correct perspective
and need never raise any hard questions.

Thank you for bullying the Congress
into complete patriotic support of your glorious leadership
providing all of the money the military asks for.

Finally, Emperor George, we are sure you are
thankful for a nation of patriotic sheep
who will follow you right over the cliff,
thankful for training our children
not to ask you any critical questions,
thankful for poets of peaceful pastoral
scenes deftly ignoring dissonance.

Thankful for patriotic youth
who will eagerly humiliate and abuse
Iraqis for your cause.

With such an Emperor and his sheep
we are invincible, and truly blessed!
Even if he wears no clothes.

Would We Kill Him Again in 2004?

On the occasion of this national holiday,
trying to remember the life of
Rev. Martin Luther King, Jr.,
I am led to witness:

Were he alive today, we would find cause
to kill him again in 2004.

This man did not die because he led
his people against racial injustice,
as horrible as that was.

He did not die because he caused
Washington to reluctantly respond
to obvious injustice and violation
of the human rights of non-whites
in the South and the North.

He died because, as he grew
in his understanding of the
evil of violence, he made

the inevitable connection
between domestic
racial violence,
continuing
poverty,
and the way
America does her usual
business using violence
in foreign affairs; draining
our economy and young lives
to line the pockets of the already rich.

King called the church (and by
the church I mean the
people of God)
from a
Birmingham
jail to take their
Jesus from beyond the stars
and to put him into their hearts.
and then, "Come on down!"
This, in itself, was a revolution,
unsettling to the comfortable church.
He called the church to ***practice***
a racial justice that the
scriptures proclaimed and
their pastors should be
proclaiming every Sunday morning.

But that is not why we killed him.

When the church invited him to witness
in the prestigious NY Riverside Church
he again became the prophet calling
this same church to honor that
same Jesus who had led
them in the South.

Because of his growth in understanding
of the power of non-violence, led
by the Satyagraha of Gandhi
as shared by Bayard Rustin
and its congruence with
his historical Jesus
he proclaimed
his truth.
This truth shook the foundations of
how America has done business
since the time of our revolution:

He condemned our culture of violence,
practiced first by cave dwellers and
still unquestioned by the Pentagon
as a curse that would lead
to the death of this great
nation and its church.

He pointed out in that seminal sermon
how Vietnam was a giant hoax
in which our "great" leaders
were bankrupting our
resources to feed
a military industrial
complex (sound familiar?)
destined to fail because only
non-violence can find loving answers.
We killed him because he challenged
our most cherished assumptions:
"***Through the use of violence***
we can bring about justice."
The first and only commandment
of the war college—what Gandhi
called, "The law of the brute."

He proclaimed, what every American
was seeing on TV, that the war
in Vietnam was not just

destroying a poor people
and their countryside
it was also destroying
the values we were
supposed to be
defending.

It seems one of the things he gained
from this now famous witness
was the enmity of the President,
Lyndon B. Johnson, who, like
President Bush,
could not stomach
opposition
to his war.

Yet, today in 2004,
polls report that Republicans
and too many Democrats support
Bush's unilateral war and even
today are afraid to agree
with King's assessment
of violence containing
its own reward.

This is why the Democrats must find
a centrist candidate to beat Bush.
They must not appear to be
saying what King said
that our unquestioning
patriotic children
(now over 500 lost)
plus the destruction
of the Iraq countryside
and people all died in vain in
order to satisfy our corporate greed.

A witness too horrible for proud, patriotic
and grieving families to contemplate.

Prophets are never popular people.
Just ask Jesus, Gandhi,
and King.

This is why we killed him and, I fear why,
in our blind, patriotic
fundamentalism
we would
kill him again
today.

Hail Caesar!

This morning a Congressperson
referred proudly to the President
as a "conqueror."

I wondered, as my soul shuddered,
if this was just another
political faux pas
like "crusade?"

I suspect not. Patriots who enable
a leader drunk with power
find such titles
easier and
easier to
say.

Just as those who enable alcoholics
look for justifications to
excuse enabling
behavior which
keeps the

addict in
sauce.

A conqueror is a leader who wages
preemptive war gladly. He
cares not the cost
in money or
mortality.

Alexander the "Great,"
Roman emperors,
Genghis Khan,
Adolph Hitler,
Idi Amin
all favored preemptive war.

They took on countries or
peoples whose resources
they wanted for
a rock-bottom
price.
They worshiped violence to
meet their needs caring
not one whit for the
needs of others.

They waged their preemptive war
on the basis of hatred and fear.
They found scapegoats to
justify genocide.

Just as those who lived in luxury
in Rome, we will praise the
conquering heros as they
parade down the street
next 4th of July.

They think they, not Bandar, made sure
oil will be available at the
cheapest possible
price.

As the crowds cheer the returning
conquerors, there are others
who weep as their sons
and daughters
are lost.

B & B have conquered Iraq.
Hail Caesar!
It is perplexing why Jesus
preferred the title,
"suffering servant?"
Did he know something George
doesn't know?

Hurry! We don't want to be
late for the parade!

Misperception

My understanding of God leads me
to affirm life, especially those
lives lived serving others.

The suicide bomber, assured by a cleric
this act of sacrifice will gain certain
entry to heaven is wrong.
Yet another lie of war.

It is much more likely on that end-day
as is perfectly clear in the Qu'rán
we shall be judged by our acts
of charity against our acts
of evildoing.

The taking of human life, especially
lives of the innocent, is not
praised in the Qu'rán
just as it was
rejected by
Jesus.

I suspect the Rabbi would also say
that killing others has little
support in the Torah.
The sixth commandment
still stands even in the face
of provocation. God's laws have
precedence over the laws of man.

The patriotic warrior, be he in
Palestine, Israel, Iraq or the USA
needs to have his moral vision checked
if he thinks that killing another, his brother,
will earn him a place in God's house.

The Pope was right, This is not a moral war;
but then, in spite of what they teach
at the war college,
no war is a moral war.

The Rain/Reign of Compassion

Visiting our victorious troops in Iraq
Donald Rumsfeld outlined the new
history that will be taught at the
war college.

He praised the soldier's precision and
accuracy, speed and mobility.
Finally, almost as an afterthought,
he praised their compassion.

Whoa!
Did I miss something here?

I saw the "shock and awe," bombs bursting in
air and underground.
I saw the government buildings turned to rubble.
I saw many other civilian areas
also turned to rubble.

I saw us destroy the Iraqi infrastructure
so that clean water and electricity were
unavailable

I have watched, helpless, as for a number of years we have
starved Iraqi children and elderly.

I watched as a whole country was plunged into anarchy

I and the world watched as criminals looted
their national museum
while our troops looked on.

I saw pathetic pictures of local hospitals overwhelmed
by battle related injuries.

I watched as we slowly counted our soldiers killed reach 100
and then climb inexorably beyond

I realized that no one was
counting the numbers of Iraqi dead or wounded
especially not the collateral damage.

I wept with joy as our few POWs were rescued and eventually
returned to their families
I wept as their POWs were transported to Cuba to be
interrogated and held without trial or any
respect for human rights.

I keep waiting for coalition forces to find any
weapons of mass destruction
UN inspectors did not already know
about and were in the process of
destroying.

I watched with sadness the confirmation that our campaign
to destroy a whole country to find, if not kill,
one man has been successful.

I have watched Rumsfeld himself implicated in the
command decision to humiliate and abuse
Iraqi civilians in prisons.

But I have seen bloody little activity
that could be called "compassion."

Unless it could be seen in the
freeing up of Iraqi oil fields
so that we can guzzle again
at the cheapest possible price
and help pay for our devastation.

One of the many lies of war concerns
using language in totally
contradictory ways so
your yea means nay
and your nay
means yea.

Only when we understand what
devastation we have visited
on Iraq and our lies to
justify our success will
we begin to understand
why they want us to go
and hate us so.

Wasteful War

War is so very wasteful.
We produce and stockpile
weapons we daren't use else
everything on earth would die.

But the R & D and then the
production and then the secure
storage cost billions.

Even conventional weapons,
airplanes, helicopters, tanks,
bunker busting bombs
cost billions to produce
and billions to maintain
and replace after using.

New "secret" satellites that
can guide our weapons
with awesome if
deadly accuracy
don't come cheap.

And the lovely computers!
Built into every airplane,
tank, and bomb
to ensure deadly
precision even
if the target is
friendly or civilian.

Funny how our technology
cannot look into the heart
of its target to discern
whether friend or foe
loving or revolting.

The cost is the same whether
we obliterate a warrior
or make a mistake
putting yet another
tiny tot in a tomb.

When protestors exercise
their 1st amendment rights in America
it is costly to protect all to
keep anger within bounds.

When Iraqis protest and shots are fired
it costs less to return the fire
killing guilty and innocent alike.
How do you calculate this waste?
The loss of American and Iraqi lives?
It is paid by the occupying power
and the Iraqi people

We have the wonderful weapons
to destroy their water and sewage
plants turning cities into sites
of public health nightmares.

Now, we are having to rebuild
these and other public utilities
we could have chosen to not
destroy in the first place.
A considerable
cost saving.

We have destroyed the capacity
of a country to feed themselves.
In the face of our corporate guilt we must
now feed a whole people at least
up to welfare standards. For
how many years? This is
a very costly business.

Bush asks for billions ignoring the fact
we are already paying billions
for the debts incurred in past wars.

In addition to his billions
for this tiny war we will have to
pay more billions to rearm
and rebuild our military
infrastructure to be ready
for his next unilateral war.

And who will pick up the tab?
You and me, kiddo, you and me.

It's Simple, Really

The biomass in the seas
keeps our oxygen high
and keeps the carbon
compressed at the seabed.

This, in turn, gives our
intergallactic period a long life
(that period between ice-ages).

Now we are over-fishing the seas
and destroying much of the
other biomass of the seas
caught in nets,
some over 30 miles long.

As the fish and biomass
are destroyed, the carbon
over produces carbon
dioxide which brings
on the next ice-age
super fast as time goes.

It bothers me
about our politicians and
those of other countries—
(they being the best
that money can buy)

They may have money but
they don't understand
the simple things.
on which life
depends.

They are too busy fighting
Iraqis while terror swims
in the back door. Terror
of human making
which, beyond a
certain threshold,
cannot be reversed.

Exceptionalism or Imperialsm?

Poetic thoughts about "U.S. Exceptionalism vs. Human Solidarity" by Kieth Helmuth in Friend's Journal, June, 2003, pp.6–8.

Exceptionalism or Imperialism?
Two names to describe the same thing.
In essence a quest for empire.

A most disturbing syndrome developing in Washington
A "Master Culture" attitude not dissimilar to Germany
before and during the reign of Adolph Hitler.

The events of 9/11 playing into the hands of George Bush
and the Pentagon and their claims for
"natural rights of domination."

Certain facets of Exceptionalism hold sway today
by Bush's attack on
Afghanistan and Iraq.

The institutionalization and constant presence of warfare.
An enclave strategy toward environmental and other threats—
no proactive preventive approach or systemic problem solving.
Build up our military world-wide to meet the
inevitable crises to protect our interests.

Can we not recognize the threats for what they are—
the rich vs. the poor,
the healthy and well-fed vs those at health risk who are poor.

Advantages for development flow to the rich,
only in a trickle down sense may, someday,
reach the poor.

The alternative is human solidarity
expressed well during the time immediate
before we invaded Iraq.

People around the world expressed
articulate opposition to Bush
and his unilateral war.

The U.S. military's rejection of human solidarity;
in its place keeping "the rights of domination"
or "might makes right" is a dark mark
for a democracy supposedly
based on justice.

And friends, it pits the religions of the world
as counterpoint to this country
we assert to be "under God."

For years human solidarity has been the focal point
for human hope by building a strong UN,
building a strong International Court,
central to all religious faiths containing ethics
of inclusion, sharing, healing and compassion.

The queries are clear:
Can God's people keep human solidarity in central focus?
Can God's people work for public policies that advance
equity,
justice,
cooperation,
peace, and
the integrity of creation?
Can God's people make these the issues of the campaign—
not just for 2004 but for all time?

War-time Casualties

The first casualty of war is truth.
Other casualties of war include:
Warriors from both sides,
Courageous public officials of peace
willing to stand against the war.
Peaceful patriots, like poets.
Civilians killed by mistake,
civilians killed by design,
civilians imprisoned but suspect—
now humiliated and abused.
A peaceful economic system,
an effective United Nations,
State Department diplomacy,
an effective world court,
an independent media,
constitutional guarantees of free speech,
protections against a government
wanting to stifle dissent;
independent poetry at the White House,
domestic programs of peace.

These casualties of war
we cannot lay at the feet of Sadaam Hussein
as Bush started the war
against the advice of most of
the rest of the world.

War-time casualties are greater
than just the bodies in uniform.
War rends the very fabric
of our nation.
raising the question of
how we can pretend
to make way for democracy in Iraq
when we litter the landscape
with casualties of our own democracy
as we litter the landscape with
the corpses of Iraqis.

Contemporary Crucifixion

"Bless the Lord, you his angels, who excel in
strength, who do His word.
Heading the voice of His word. Bless the Lord,
all you His hosts,
You ministers of His, who do His pleasure.
Bless the Lord, all His works. In all places of
His dominion. Bless the Lord, O my soul!"
—Psalm 103::20–22

We are doing it again
As Jesus came before Pilate, he was asked, "What is truth?"
The personification of God's truth stood before him,
in silence, his life a testimony to truth.

There are contemporary followers of this inclusive truth of love
who offered up their bodies as human shields
to try to deter the madness of war in Iraq.
Now they are being hauled before a modern Pilate
by the Treasury Department. for witnessing to God's truth:
"we are all members of God's family
and family members do not
kill one another."

I expect they will be fined and imprisoned for their
love of a brother.
Does it give us any pause to know that 2,100 years ago
they would likely have been crucified by
the side of the Christ?

I thank God for such ministers as are willing to stand
beside the children of Iraq in an attempt
to shield them from our bombs.
Be with them, Lord, as they
stand beside You in front
of our new Pilate.

If Mr. Rogers Were President

A good friend, Harold Miller, wrote me in these
scary and dreary times and mused
what the world would be like if Mr. Rogers
(of TV fame) were the President.

An interesting thought, that.
Though I can't stretch my imagination
enough to imagine his changing his shoes
in front of a visiting ambassador.

But I can see him taking long walks
much to the consternation of the Secret Service (SS),
into South-east DC until he encounters a poor black
and hungry youngster who does not know his dad
and whose mom works two jobs.
I can see him inviting the child
to the Rose Garden for tea
and making sure the SS
invites his mom as well.

I can see him walking through
the oncology ward at Children's
Hospital, singing with and
for these children,
bald and bereft
of hope.
I can see him making the generals wait
as he helps an elderly woman who
is finding it hard to live on her
meager social security.

I can see him sponsoring bills to
provide for universal health care,
not on the basis of the ability
to pay but on health need.

I can see him finding the money
for this and other humane
legislative priorities by
telling the Pentagon
to get used to it,
they will have to expect a 90%
reduction to their budget in the future.

I can hear him gleefully announce
to super-patriotic audiences that
if they are dissatisfied with his
allocation of funds for the military
they need to organize neighborhood bake sales
and donate the profits to the Pentagon.

I can hear him suggest,
(tongue in cheek?), that they offer
bagels for bullets,
granola for grenades,
cakes for cruisers,
apple pies for aircraft.

His cabinet aghast at his
smiling humor,
I suspect he would sleep well
having provided funds
for AIDs orphans
and food for
famine relief
But it will not likely happen as
it takes millions to run for President
and Mr. Rogers wore well-worn shoes,
indicative of his income.

Besides, I expect if by chance the
imagination of the electorate was engaged,
as might well have happened had Martin run for President,
the power of the dark and evil ones
would make sure that Mr. Rogers
would become just another brick
in the American Wailing Wall of
those good liberals who all died
within the lifetime of Mr. Rogers
abruptly,
prematurely,
mysteriously.

Warheads, Warheads

There are warheads and then
there are warheads.

The warheads on the ends of missiles
are somewhat easy to deal with.
They are a particular size so
their damage is predictable.

They are costly and you can measure
their cost by the number of schools
that will not be built or the number
of new cancer patients as the money
for R & D is tied up in warheads.
Eventually we end up paying for
the schools and R & D as well
but this raises the deficit and
shifts the cost of the warheads
onto our grandchildren.

Everyone building warheads pays
an intolerable price taken out of
the backs of their people

Osama bin Laden, George Bush,
Sadaam Hussein or Tony Blair.
They buy warheads with the
people's money, mortgaging
their futures.

Then there are the warheads
that sit on the shoulders of
our respected heads of state.
These are infinitely harder to
deal with as they are very
unpredictable. And, of course,
they are much more costly
and can do infinitely more
damage than the mechanical
warheads.

Osama bin Laden, warhead,
caused the destruction of the
Twin Towers, part of the Pentagon
and four civilian airliners.
This resulted in the destruction
of Afghanistan and possibly
his life as a warhead
outside of dark tunnels.

Sadaam Hussein, also a
warhead, thumbed his nose
at George and the UN.
Now his country lies in ruins
and he is looking for part—
time work as a spider.

George Bush, also a warhead,
has a vastly greater arsenal than the other warheads
and managed to wipe their noses in the dirt
proving, once again, "might makes right."

Now he says he wants peace
between Israel and Palestine.

But the Israelis also have warheads
who imitated our White House warhead
managing to shred the roadmap for peace for
the foreseeable future.
The Palestinians retaliated
(what did the warheads expect?)
And here we go again,
Watch the roadmap blow away
as it has done many times before.

If warhead Bush had such good
intelligence about warhead Hussein's
weapons of mass destruction, why is
he still sending people to Iraq to find them?
Was the "need": for this unilateral war
wise, necessary, or contrived?

Warheads don't make peace,
warheads make war; warheads kill
That's all they are good for.

It's past time to remove the warhead
from the White House before.
he kills us all.

Testing

This is a test of the
Emergency Sanity System
This is only a test

If you are a human
created by a higher power,
move on, move on.

If you love your neighbor
as you love yourself,
move on, move on.

If your neighbor is hungry
and you feed her as yourself,
Move on, move on.

If your neighbor is cold
and you share your winter coat,
Move on, move on.

If your neighbor is ill
and you make sure a doctor comes,
Move on, move on.

If your neighbor dies a sudden death
and you make sure his kids are cared for
as you hope he would your own,
move on, move on.

If a tornado devastates a few and you join
with the neighbors many to make the future bright for all,
Move on, move on.
Will you live such a life, move on,
if you neighbor's black, brown or white?
Move on, move on.

And where do you draw the line?
When is a neighbor no longer a neighbor?
When is family no longer family?
When are we encouraged to hate?

I want to know how a professing
Christian or Moslem can justify the
destruction of 66,000 civilian lives
in Hiroshima or 3,000 lives in
the World Trade Center?
NOTHING justifies such actions.
Do we not have leaders willing to admit
developing a nuclear weapon was wrong
but using it on a civilian target worse?

Osama bin Laden attacked the
Twin Towers in an insane act
but he was not the first.

If we cannot be sane, then
anything goes, and everything will.
No neighbor can be trusted
Religious morality a sham.

If you wake up scared and afraid,
there are damn good reasons.
Go back to sleep

This is a test of the
Emergency Sanity System
and we may have all flunked.

Good thing
it was only a test.
With forgiveness offered
there is still hope

Sanity requires recognition of sin
willingness to ask for forgiveness
willingness to stand under judgment.
willingness to walk away from violence
Only then can we move on,

"In God there is no East or West
In Her no South or North
But one great fellowship of love
throughout the whole wide earth;
all children of the living God
are surely kin to me."
The basis of our sanity.

There will be
another test of the
Emergency Sanity System.
Be Prepared.

Justification by Action

The 5th Law of Violence

Jimmy Carter, in his book
Living Faith justifies our dropping
the A-bomb on Hiroshima.
At least he has the good grace
to admit that most Japanese
disagree with his justifications.

The first excuse, espoused by Truman himself,
was the belief that much greater invasion
casualties were avoided.

Tell that to the Most High:
"Japanese lives are less precious
than American lives."
"Seyz who?" God. responds.

The second justification is only a little less chauvinist,
"The horror of its devastation makes future use less likely."
The reality of its horror has not stopped our scientists
from developing A and H bombs
much more lethal in great quantity.

We and others now have enough weapons of mass destruction
to extinguish life, all life on the earth, 10 times over.
An insane policy appropriately entitled,
Mutually Assured Destruction (MAD).

Humanity is just waiting for some dumb warhead
living in the White House or a rogue bomber
to push the wrong button and then say, "Oops!"
There will not be time for apologies.
Such a mistake will not be tolerated
but still, Armageddon will ensue
with no excuses possible.

What Makes a War Criminal?

In an interview reported on NPR,
Robert McNamara admitted that had America lost WW II,
he, and many others of our leaders
would have been tried as war criminals.
Tried for the fire-bombing of Tokyo,
the bombing of Hiroshima and
the bombing of Nagasaki
in which the primary
victims were
civilians.

He also asserted that he did not know any
military commander in combat who
had not made errors of judgment
that resulted in the loss of lives
of their own troops or others.

On this observation, he based his present
opposition to weapons of mass extinction
". . . as errors will always happen."
And in a nuclear war, an error

could easily wipe out
an entire nation.

But the winner of that war would never
have to face an international
tribunal, being accused of
crimes against humanity;
being a war criminal.

I guess this is why George Bush declared
victory while our soldiers continue to
die daily. He did not want to be
accused of crimes against
humanity.

Winning is everything. Only those who lose
get tried as war criminals.

How very different it will be
when we stand before God and
our judgment will not be determined
by who won and who lost
but by how we played the game.

An Enraged Christ

Try to explore your own feelings after reading "Hiroshima, Military Voices of Dissent" found on the ecapc.org website.

Certain Biblical passages
give me pause such as Christ
driving the money changers
from the temple
with a whip.

It is such a contrast to the man of peace
who walked the shores of Galilee
healing the sick,
even on the
Sabbath.

If Paul Tillich is right, then we are a nation filled
with money changers who worship the
profit we gain by using violence
to dominate and destroy others.
Our ultimate concern

We worship a world of people and corporations
who traffic in violence, with slogans saying,
"We never forget who our friends are."

On August 6th as we remember our dropping of the bomb
on Hiroshima and Nagasaki, let us hear other voices:

Admiral Leahy wrote in 1950
"This barbarous weapon was of no material
assistance in the war."
"The Japanese were already defeated and ready to surrender."
and he continued in his memoirs . . .
"In being the first to use it we adopted an ethical standard
common to the barbarians of the Dark Ages."
This White House Chief of Staff and
Chairman of the Joint Chiefs closed his writing asserting,
"Wars cannot be won destroying
women and children."
General Dwight Eisenhower recalled telling Secretary of War,
Henry Stimson, he opposed using the bomb on two counts:
"The Japanese were ready to surrender,"
and "We should not be the first nation
to ever use it."

Admiral William Halsey said in 1946
"The . . . bomb was an unnecessary experiment."
"Japan had put out many peace feelers through Russia
long before we used it."

Not all Pacific war veterans applauded using it!
Marine Corp Sargeant Joe O'Donnel, retired, said,
"To drop a bomb on women, children and the elderly,
I draw a line there and
I still hold it."

Rescue Pilot, Doug Dowd, Pacific Theater said,
"It was clear the Japanese had lost the ability to
defend themselves

and were suing for peace through Russia
long before Hiroshima."

Major Ed Everts, Army Air Corps said, dropping the bomb
"was a war crime for which our leaders
should have been put on trial
as were the German and
Japanese leaders."

Not bloody likely, as we won!

These were honest men of war, not men of peace.
If they told the truth, which has been supported by many others,
then I can envision a Christ with his whip, striding
through the Temple of this nation to
drive out those many who profited
by killing God's innocent Japanese
children and those who continue
to profit in
our war in
Iraq.
Hey, my Christian right-wing fundamentalist brothers,
You think only Osama bin Laden and his
right-wing Moslem fundamentalists hate?
Beware, an enraged Christ!

The Voices of Hibakusha

Inspired by an article by Courtland Milloy,
"The Enola Gay in a Truly Terrifying Light,"
—The Washington Post, 12/17.03, p.B1

A few survivors of our terrorist attacks on
Hiroshima and Nagasaki
came to our new war museum.
They saw there the plane, a B-29
that dropped the atom bomb
on Hiroshima, the Enola Gay,
and this is what one said:

"I was 13 when this plane crossed the sky
above my school yard. It looked so small.
Then I was blown off the ground
my skin peeling off—I was angry and in pain.
I saw my classmates on fire all around me
and I wondered, What is going on?"

Minoro Nishino also asked other unanswered questions.
"Can you please explain why a pilot would put
his mother's name on such an airplane?

In Japan, mothers and sweethearts
represent life and love,
not war and death"

Hiroshima lost 100,000 people by
this one bomb and in Nagasaki,
by another, 60,000 perished—
most all who died were
innocent civilians
Just like the Twin Towers.

Teumi Tanaka was also 13 but he was in Nagasaki.
Now 71 he said:
"It was so sad. I felt the tears
start to come down, Seeing all your
fighter planes on display I realize this is a war museum.
What we need are more peace museums."
Hirotami Yamada was 14 that
fateful morning on his school playground.
He remembers a blinding flash, intense heat.
People not killed outright, died of radiation—
Hirotami lost his whole family.
"I did not hear or see the plane,
so I had no idea why everything was on fire.
Now I see this plane that killed my family."

Tamiko Tomonaga was 16, became a nurse
and believes she was spared, a Hibakusha,
to tell this story:
". . . to let the voices of the others
be heard, to give their testimony
and help bring about a world
without such weapons."

Today, eight countries
have nuclear weapons,
forty more countries
have the ability
to quickly produce them.

These Hibakusha correctly call them
"weapons of mass extinction."
They should know.

Listen America, listen,
listen world, listen,
to these terrified
screaming
crying
children
who were
our targets in 1945.

They still grieve, speak and weep.
Will they have died in vain?
Listen.

Rules to Live By

This President has given us and our children some very clear rules to live by, his actions taking precedence over his words.

Might Makes Right
when world opinion is opposed
to his unilateral war and
he can't show any good
reason to go to war
we go anyway
because . . .
Might Makes Right

To the Victor Go the Spoils
War has been about conquest since
time began. If Iraq had not had
exceedingly rich oil fields
we would not be there.
We are there
because . . .
To the Victor Go the Spoils

The Ends Justify the Means
We will use the most terrifying bombs
destroying a small country's
infrastructure, starving
its children and abusing
and humiliating its citizens
while never charging them
with any crime in a court of law
because . . .
The Ends Justify the Means

The President as Commander and Chief is Always Right
The President can lie about weapons of mass destruction
The President can lie about Al Qaeda in Iraq
The President can support Rumsfeld
because water runs uphill.
We dare not blame the
chain of command
because . . .
The President as Commander and
Chief is Always Right

Anything to Win

This is war culture
in which anything goes.
Our own sons and daughters
offered up as cannon fodder, filling
a centerfold in the Washington Post—
those lives lost in the month of April 2004
while Rumsfeld admitted on this very same day
there was no proven connection between Al Qaeda
and the war in Iraq and still no weapons of mass destruction.

Meanwhile, this same beautiful spring day, we woke up to
chilling photographs displayed of naked Iraqi civilians
being humiliated and tortured in the very prison
Sadaam Hussein used for similar bestiality.
Torture by our own occupation forces
embedded with the CIA.

These should be yet two more nails in the Bush coffin
but this administration has become so immune
to anything remotely resembling morality
that all they can do is to promise
to prosecute the lad who

was so disturbed by
his and others' actions
he told the world.

This is it, folks: war culture
where anything goes.

That Close

With appreciation for the FCNL white paper
"At the Crossroads: Disarmament or Re-Nuclearization"

In 1995 as we were workcamping in Romania,
the USA and Norway launched a research rocket
Within seconds it had triggered Russia's
early warning system and Boris Yeltsin
came within minutes of launching
a nuclear war on us.

He only stopped when
Russian radar determined the rocket
was going out to sea rather than toward
the USSR.

That was close.

We can better imagine the reality of Hiroshima and Nagasaki
after the events of 9/11 if we will learn from history.
The attack against our homeland was minuscule
compared with what we did to Japan in 1945.
The violence we have willingly visited on the world

as the best way of conflict resolution
is finally coming home.

We are at a crossroads
and vigorous action to change the course
of our national ship of state is required as we
never, no never want to come
that close to the abyss
again.

Please God, please! Bring us back
into touch with the reality of
your peace and grant us all
a world without end,
Amen.

Defining Our Future

I do not usually find truth
in the statements of those
advertising proudly instruments of
destruction and death. But the slogan
of Northrup Grumman, proudly proclaiming
on TV and in full-page ads in the Washington Post
they are "Defining Our Future"
rings all too true.

We teach violence
as the best way to solve problems,
maintain a nuclear arsenal and a constant
threat to life as we know it; flood our cities with
guns and proudly train our youth in the military
to play devastating video games with
real live human targets but
deceptively appearing
only as blips on a
radar screen.

Then we wonder
why the world has changed

to where everyone is a suspect.
Where everyone else seems to hate us;
where we have to have our feet and shoes
inspected, not for athlete's foot fungus but for C-4,
before we can fly to Grandma's house; where our
soldiers and defense contractors are murdered
and their bodies paraded in the streets.
Get real, folks! Who has
defined our future?

And who allowed them
to do so?

Unprovoked

This morning old/new deadly news
Six British soldiers killed in Iraq
in an "unprovoked attack.".
I rage at the abuse of language
by reporterrs who should know better
almost as much as the abuse of truth
and the systematic abuse of a country

Having destroyed their country,
infrastructure, people, hopes and dreams
What more devastation merits
provocation?

Yet Another Lie

Why am I not surprised?
King George lied to us
in his State of the Union speech.

Someone else will take the fall
but George knew four months
prior that it was a lie.
He lied anyway.

Does the President assume
a time of war is a time of
deceit? Does he assume
all good patriots will
listen and not question;
line up to die for his lie?

Not this patriot.

Glee in Killing

I am amazed we can take such glee
in killing two admitted despots
Ursay and Uday.

I would not be adverse to have seen
them spend their lives in prison
for crimes against humanity.
The rule of law affirmed.

To say nothing about the real
intelligence about the sites
of possible weapons
of mass destruction
now lost forever.

Forgive my cynicism but
it is terribly convenient
to not have them say,
there were no secret
weapons sites.

If anyone could have told the world
the truth about Iraqi weapon
capabilities and secret sites
beyond any doubt it was Ursay.
Our dancing in glee on his grave
obscures the reality he was
much more valuable to
us alive rather
than dead.
Unless, of course, he would have
confirmed B & B lied to their people
as well as to the world;
in which case, let the
celebration continue
far into the night!

Forgive me if I sit this one out.

A Prayer for Forgiveness

To God we can no longer pray,
"Father, forgive us,
for we know not what we do,"
because we do know
and went to war knowing
it was a violation of every thing
Jesus taught, lived and died for.

Target: Peacemakers

Yesterday,
another bomb went off in Baghdad.
Not just any bomb.
This one targeted the UN offices
housing peacemakers
from many countries:
killing the chief UN envoy to Iraq,
Killing the head of UNICEF,
killing about 17 and
injuring 100 others.

One of the hardest things
for Bush to understand
is how war breeds tyrants.
who commit new atrocities.
I understand the suffering servant.
I understand crucifixion.
I understand those willing to
risk their lives for peace.

I guess the message is clear but grim.
There are those who will use
our war and occupation
as an organizing tool.
They say to the world,
"We will kill any and all Americans;
we will also kill all those
who are their friends.
we will make your sacrifices so costly
you will all go home,
as you had to do in Vietnam."

We have no one to blame but ourselves.
Had we heeded
the will of the world's people,
had we agreed to continue
to work with UN weapons inspectors,
had we not bombed the bejesus
out of Baghdad and the rest of Iraq,
we would not have offered the people
a splendid organizing tool
turning bitter Iraqis into
tenacious patriots.

Part of what we mean
with our signs and bumper stickers,
"War is not the answer" is precisely this:
through war, Bush and Blair have managed
to create the monsters they were supposedly hunting.
Iraqis who see anyone supporting an American—
made peace as enemies worthy of death

So my prophesy is the killing will continue,
not just of soldiers, but of peacemakers as well.
This war costing 100 billion
and thousands of lives,
including those of the
peacemakers,
will not go away
and no amount of

patriotism, fear,
or spin (read lies)
by B & B
will make it
go away.

We may have killed Sadaam Hussein and his family
but others will rise to take their place.
And no Iraqi government serving
at the will of America or now
the UN will be tolerated,

We have made enemies out of a people we have
terrorized and tried to bomb back
to the Stone Age.

We may be able to help them rebuild
but only after we have gone home.
Another paradox to live with.

Under Judgment

"Do not think yourself better because you burn up friends and enemies with long-range missiles without ever seeing what you have done"

—Thomas Merton

Modern warriors kill from afar
murder, maim, obliterate,
destroying friends and
enemies alike.

The Mennonites and the
Carter Center tell us we kill
ten civilians: elderly, women,
and children for every soldier
we kill in Iraq.

Surely if there is a God
and Jesus is his Son,
we will stand under judgment
and our brilliant technology

won't help us assault heaven
then or now.

Christ is concerned with choices.
No one has to go to war.
But when you choose to
launch the missile,
you choose
death over life,
you choose
to be the instrument
of that death.

You choose to burn friend
and foe alike. Your choice is
not forced on you. Anyone
can say no and follow the
Christ who overcomes all wars.

Today in Iraq, water and oil spill,
flow and burn back into the sand
like the blood and water
that flowed from his side as he
asked God to forgive those
who chose to murder him.

How patient will God be with
those who choose to kill from afar?
That you do not know their names
as you destroy their future
will not save you.

I know little of an afterlife
but I do know justice
and if justice be served
then that precious child
that you just chose to kill
will someday have justice.

Hear the Psalmist,
"*You caused judgment to be heard from heaven;*
the earth feared and was still.
When God arose to judgment,
to deliver all the oppressed of the earth."†

Whether it is the sins of Sadaam
or the bombs of Bush
only God can deliver
the oppressed.

But, I am concerned about you, soldier!
Now, before it is too late,
learn to fear and be still;
make the right choices,
for God's sake.

† *Psalm 76:8,9.*

Physical Laws of Motion

Is it just possible
that if we had learned
our lessons in high school physics
and then applied them as a metaphor
to living lives in congruence with
nature that we might not be
having to memorialize
the tragedy of 9/11?

Jesus stated this law
in spiritual terms but right on
target for 9/11: "Those who live by
the sword will die by the sword."

"Wait", you cry,
acting hurt and angry,
"What did we do to deserve
such a despicable attack on the
Twin Towers?"

Perhaps deserving is the wrong word.
Perhaps predictable is a better word.

Our School of the Americas,
providing billions to Israel in its
war on Palestine; providing arms
and munitions and training
to Osama bin Laden and
Sadaam Hussein and
many other dictators
and tyrants.

Is bound to be **predictable** in its action
to an equal and opposite reaction;
basic high school physics class.

I wonder if during class George
was making paper airplanes
and dreaming of an American Empire
rather than learning lessons useful
to live lives in congruence with nature
and with our brother?

Perhaps we should use this time of
9/11 memorial and think creatively
how we can reclaim the dream
of brother King rather than
trying to maintain our
hegemony in the
Middle East.

People in this fine country
showed the world, in our lifetime,
how to bring about justice and
transform a hateful southern culture
without using arms and weapons,
without devastating the infrastructure
of a whole country. Clearly they
understood the physical
laws of motion and

applied it to the
human family.

Was George making paper airplanes
then as well? He certainly was not sitting in.
If he and the Pentagon had learned any lessons from
the Civil Rights Movement, it is possible that the despicable
attacks on the Twin Towers and the Pentagon
might never have occurred.

They're still making airplanes and bombs.
and making us pay for them
and the world they produce.

The Truth Will Out

September 25, 2003

On tonight's news
America's chief weapon's inspector, David Kay,
admitted they have found not one weapon
of mass destruction
in Iraq.

He asserts
they have had unfettered access,
they have been able to interview
all manner of Iraqi scientists,
they have the most sophisticated
monitoring and search equipment
in our intelligence arsenal.

Yet they have found
Not one weapon of mass destruction.
Not one weapon
Not one

Exactly the finding of the Bush—
despised UN weapons inspectors
exactly one war ago.

Sometimes in my despair
over this unnecessary war waged to
find those weapons of mass
destruction Bush "knew"
were there, it is
a bitter consolation
to know truth prevails

the question persists,
is anybody listening?

This poem won the Editor's Choice Award of Poetry.com and the International Library of Poetry. August, 2004

September 28, 2003

Today is the birthday of Confucius,.
the wise teacher of ancient China.
It is clear, if you know his teachings,
that such wisdom is still in
very short supply.

*"Do you want to know what knowledge is?
When you know something, recognize you know it,
and when you don't know something,
recognize that you don't know it.
That's knowledge. "†*

We could have avoided a costly, wasted war
had Bush listened to the UN weapons inspectors
who clearly said they had found no
weapons of mass destruction.

Today, exactly one war later, Bush's own
weapons inspector reported exactly the same.

---

† *The Analects of Confucious, Book 2, Chapter 17.*

Had Bush the humility to admit he did not know
we could have avoided this terrible war.
Happy birthday, old sage.

Turning the Tide

Dedicated to Colman McCarthy
working with the tide of God's power

Watch children building sand castles
at low tide; magnificent structures grow.
But no matter the protective moat
dug to protect the edifice,
the power of the moon's
gravity, like God's love,
also an invisible force,
wins the day and
wipes the beach
clean. "Ufufuo."[1]

Humanity, a part of this same natural world,
can build sandy structures with violence
but cannot turn the tides of God.
Racism, slavery, sexism,
war buillt structures
doomed to fail.

Now, our government is building an edifice of empire
to feed the greed of the Energy Emperor and
the oil oligarchy that wages war in Iraq
while challenging the tide of
worldwide multi-nationalism
which like God's love and
justice, will not be denied.

Racism still persists, in spite of slavery's demise—
We live in an imperfect world, the need for
daily cleansing tides made manifest.
But will we deny that slavery
was wrong? Continue to
build medieval castles
in the Iraqi sand?

The United Nations is far from perfect; made
less so when we refuse our dues. But
the tide of One Human Family
struggling to live together
in peace will not
be denied.

Can One Human Family develop a constitution
based on peace, sharing and protecting
earth's resources with justice and
liberty for ALL?

Who can deny the power of the tide?
Must God's adult children still
build castles on the sand?
What gives you hope?
Working against or
with the tide?

---

[1] *Ufufuo, Swahili meaning rebirth, recovery, rebuilding and reconciliation.*

Truth as a Testimony

To most of us, truth is a value
we teach our children. As one of
the Ten Commandments it has
always had a pretty high priority.

But all of us are aware that lying
is a common reality. Used car
salesmen and politicians rank
high among those from whom
we expect untruthfulness.

Sir Winston Churchill called it
"terminological inexactitude,"
when regularly practiced by
government politicians.

But a lie is a lie is a lie.

Truth is the mortar that binds all of us together in
One Human Family. It is the only bonding agent
ever discovered enabling men and women
to live as husband and wife,

enabling siblings to live
together in family,
enabling neighbor to live
side by side with neighbor.

Community becomes a curse,
nationhood a provocation to
other nations without the healing
power of veracity.

Learning to trust does not come easily.
It is based on experiences of truth.
All it takes is one lie to break
this bond, diluting the mortar
essential to bind us together.

One of the reasons that we are today
in such a precarious way is because
we not only lie to others to gain
greedy advantage,
we lie to each other.
Cynicism is a terrible thing
but it replaces the binding
power of truth. It is the basis
of the fear we have of the other,
our attitude after being lied to
over and over again.

Friend's testimony of truth
seems anachronistic in a world
where politicians regularly lie
to the nation;
the police regularly lie
about their brutality toward minorities,
parents and teachers regularly lie
about their abuse of children.
The Air Force top brass regularly lies
about rape and assault on women,
the CEO of Enron lies about accounting.
Bush still lies about weapons of mass

destruction; a basis for his unilateral war:
A lie is a lie is a lie.

The second amendment to the constitution, the
"right" to bear arms,
seems strangely necessary when your neighbor steals
from your garden
and then lies about it. Is this instant if
primitive justice our only protection
or may truth suffice?

Is there a correlation between the rage
expressed by school children who
kill their chums and teachers
because of being treated
with shame by bullies
who have lied their way
out of responsibility
for their actions?

Perhaps the testimony of truth telling
by the Religious Society of Friends
is not quite so anachronistic
after all.

Shirin Abadi, Nobel Laureate

Judge, Shirin Abadi, lawyer,
advocate for the rights of women and children,
the first Moslem woman
to be given the Nobel
Prize For Peace.

There will be those who will object
especially in the face of Bush's claim
that Iran is a part of an axis of evil.

Meanwhile, within Iran, 53 year old
Shirin Abadi has herself suffered
because she supported human
and democratic rights for all.

There are those who have their
favorite hobby horse and are
sad when their horse does not win.

There are others within Iran who oppose
human rights for women and children and snub her award.
But then they would likely snub a Moslem

man receiving the award if he
also advocated equal rights
for women and children.

As a person who cherished women
and children, I do not doubt
that Mohammed himself
would be the first to
laud Judge Abadi.

Peace, like every other value, begins at home.
When the Islamic revolution forced Judge Abadi off the bench,
the first woman judge in Iran,
they defined themselves
by demoting her.

Alfred Nobel established the award
"to encourage dreamers!"
Dream on, Shirin Abadi!

Milestone

Today marked another milestone
in Bush's war with Iraq. Today,
as two more American soldiers were killed
the number of our sons and daughters
killed since Bush proclaimed VICTORY!
has surpassed the number that died
before he glibly lied about our conquest.

As we stumble over this new milestone
trying to understand presidential lying
Bush appeared on a carrier on which
was displayed a magnificent sign,
"Mission Accomplished." When asked
who produced this sign, Bush said
it came from the carrier personnel.
Later a White House official admitted
they had brought the sign with them.

Is it any wonder we are a cynical people
when every milestone in this
sad and oily war is marked
by a new lie straight from
the mouth of the President?

Weapons of mass destruction? (None)
Evidence of nuclear weapons? (None)
Links between Al Qaeda & Iraq? (None)
Clear CIA proof of the above? (None)
Victory? (No)
Mission Accomplished? (Hardly)
Truthful words? (Quickly recanted)

I shudder to imagine what new lie
will be offered to the world
to mark the next milestone
in Bush's "crusade", one of
the few words he chose
that was blatant
truth in this
tragic war.

A Trail of Violence

"Praise ignorance, for what man
has not encountered he has not destroyed"
—Wendell Berry, The Mad Farmer
Liberation Front.

I was stunned as I returned
from a couple of years living in Africa.
Walking up the Taquitz trail to visit
Taquitz Peak and Jeff Southwell.
I followed a trail of violence.

A new dirt parking lot at the trail head
with no thought as to the erosion
that would ensue.

Every sign on the trail
pockmarked with bullet holes.

Whole stands of Yellow Pine dead—
not from Pine Beetle but from
the gradual invasion of ozone
spreading up from the valley, our own
intimate weapon of mass destruction.

And then the bleak landscape
where a recent fire, started by arson,
had consumed virgin timber
now bowing to ozone and
just awaiting the eager flames
and voracious Santa Ana winds.

Acre after acre after acre burned
bare to the rocky soil. The fire's
heat so intense it destroyed
ancient trees down to the ground;
destroyed the humus it took nature
one thousand years to create—
all because we have regarded all fire as
hostile to nature and have created
stands of high, dry and dense tinder
just waiting for a spark that will
now destroy the timber.
Nature's fires clean the forest—
Our fires destroy the forest.

Man wants to live close to nature
building homes as a part of the forest,
bringing a foreign population and its
commerce to greedily feed,
doomed when nature finally ignites.

I am appalled
at what ignorant man has done
(encountering nature he thinks
he can dominate and control)
just in my lifetime.

I stagger up the rocky ridge to Jeff's
lookout, following this trail of violence
surveying the devastation of this
precious mountain habitat
where I grew into manhood
and the tears will not stop.

Today, in the great "super fires" of 2003
we see the power of nature to resist
our arrogant assumptions—that we
do not have to abide by the
hard lessons learned by
ancient peoples we
destroyed who
lived in harmony
with nature.

I weep for those killed fleeing the
fire storm, I have been there, closeup.
I grieve for those losing their homes
and cherished family momentos.
But I also weep for this forest biome
that is having to start life all over again
just because, in our ignorance of
nature's way, and our arrogant
greed, we created a devastation
much greater than God's nature
creates with occasional lightning.

"Hopeless" is Not in God's Vocabulary

I am not surprised
though deeply saddened
at the news, just reported,
that Iraq seriously tried to avert the war.
A top (former) Pentagon advisor, Richard Pearle,
was ordered not to pursue the deal.

Though Iraqi officials continued to deny
they had weapons of mass destruction, they
offered U.S. agencies and scientists free reign
to carry out inspections. General Habbush,
head of Iraqi intelligence and the Jack of
Diamonds in our infamous deck of cards,
also offered U.N. supervised free elections,
oil concessions to U.S. companies,
and was prepared to turn over
al Qaeda terrorist, Abdul
Rahman Yasin as a
gesture of good faith.

The CIA, told of this peace offer, refused to
meet with Iraqi officials.
Richard Pearle, architect of Bush's Iraq policy said
he was willing to meet with Iraqi officials but was ordered
by the U.S. Government not to.
The Iraqis were reportedly ready
to go anywhere to talk, to cut a deal.

In March after the American invasion began
Rumsfeld said the U.S. had done
everything humanly possible
to avoid war and to secure
Iraqi disarmament.

Everything is a very inclusive word. Clearly,
everything did not include listening to
the attempts of many credible
peacemakers to avoid war.
Bush was determined to go to war
and with unilateral arrogance he did it.
"Hopeless" clearly is a part of his vocabulary.

Curmudgeon Out of the Closet

With grudging appreciation for Jon Winokur

I admit to being a curmudgeon
and I suspect God is one too.
How would you feel if you worked
for seven days and nights, creating
the world and culminating in Adam and Eve
and then humanity spent subsequent
generations blowing the world all to hell?
Curmudgeons—
refuse to view the world through rose-colored glasses,
expect that if things can get worse by human effort, they will,
are disillusioned in that they have no illusions,
don't hate the sinner but detest their sins,
do not believe that "reality TV" is in any way real,
do not believe that youth necessarily will save us,
think that our love affair with violence will be its own reward,
do not hate George Bush any more than Adolph Hitler,
do not hate Bill Clinton and more than other popular strippers,
distrust any politician who says he/she can make things better,
distrust the widely held illusion that politicians can be benign,

are skeptical of politicians who swear to uphold a
violent constitution.
love the world but expect we will destroy it, probably
sooner than later,
know we are in Iraq for the oil and new markets,
democracy be damned,
know that "military intelligence" like "compassionate
conservatives" are oxymorons
know that TV violence is the American opiate, substituting
for any meaningful revolution,
think that most doctors, like some Quakers, start out to do
good and end up doing very well,
realize that there are in groups and out groups and curmudgeons, like
poets of substance, are always in the out groups,
love their grandchildren and hold out hope they may
improve the world
but think it's not likely,
turn their spiritual despair and political betrayal
into humor, disgust and sarcasm,
realize that our profit over arms and ammunition
sales in the world
outweigh any roadmaps for possible peace,
Can see that if "chain of command" and following the
example of the commander in chief
have any meaning in military or human language,
then the responsibility for
abuse and humiliation of Iraqi civilians we imprisoned
is shared by that whole chain of command
right up to and including Rumsfeld and Bush
by a Quaker curmudgeon.

Is this Justice?

Rain pouring and wind blowing
my neighbor's tree down on his car.

Another of these common storms
blowing up from the Carolinas
with near hurricane winds.

When Hurricane Isabel blew through
we thought we had experienced
nature's wrath but then,

A month or so later, nature gave
California and other western
states their due with
"super wildfires."

Now we are hunkered down for
another siege and I wonder
if this might just be God's
way to punish us for our
despicable actions in
Iraq.

As we catch the leaks and mop the floor,
Bush parades, smiling with the Queen and Prince Philip,
plainly enjoying playing King George where he is
appreciated more than here.

What I don't understand is,
if this terrible weather be God's justice
for George Bush's unilateral and unnecessary war,
then why are we being punished?

Just because we followed orders, killing soldiers,
civilians and too many precious children?
Just because we gave him the money
for arms and ammunition and the permission to use it?
Just because our elected representatives did not stand in the way?
Just because we let him lie to us and the world and
go to war on his own?
Come on, God, give us a break.
We didn't mean to ignore you
or your teachings or the rest
of the civilized world.

It's just that George so loves
playing "King" and hobnobbing
with the Queen that he's
not very accessible
these days.

But such is the way with all emperors
It's nigh unto impossible to get them
out of the saddle once they start
forming a posse to kill all the
bad guys even if there are
a few more than his
childish deck of cards.

So, Lord, if this be our punishment,
then so be it. You're the boss.

But I wish you would direct some of this disaster on
George himself. I'm tired of him
blaming all his failures
on peace protesters,
soldiers following orders,
faulty CIA intelligence,
Al Qaeda and the
United Nations
and getting away with it.

Lying As A Habit

The President just made a hasty trip to Iraq
to eat Thanksgiving turkey with our soldiers
and show the world how brave and daring
he is as Commander in Chief.

The trip went without a hitch
primarily because of the skillful lying
(since the plan was hatched in October)
keeping almost everyone in the dark
including the parents of the President.

You should be proud!
Our president has been lying to us since
he was smushed into office.
He has become so skilled
in presidential prevarication
that now we applaud him
for every new audacity.

Admittedly, he had to lie for reasons of security.
Funny,
if the war was the victory he proclaimed in previous lying,
it seems he would have been welcomed
throughout Iraq as a conquering hero!

Instead, he had to sneak out of America,
sneak into Iraq, and sneak back home
under the cover of
"acceptable" lies and secrecy.
Some hero!
Some victory!
Some sneaky deception!
Likely the most expensive
Thanksgiving dinner in presidential history.
and, of course, we picked up the tab.

Are you really being deluded by the trip of this turkey?

Asking the Hard Questions

It is the nature of maturity and wisdom
to be able to ask the hard questions.

Good political leaders, like good teachers,
surround themselves with those willing
to ask the hard questions.

I would like to suggest some questions—
we Quakers call them "queries,"
that I suspect no one has been willing
to ask of our more recent presidents:

"Who would Jesus bomb?"
"Who would Jesus kill?"
"Who would Jesus torture?"
"To whom did Jesus lie?"
"To whom would Jesus sell
or give away guns, ammo,
tanks, helicopters, missiles,
teaching how to use them?
"What skills of violence did

Jesus teach to his disciples?
"How did Jesus confront
those who hated him?"

I suspect these are hard questions
because the answers are so obvious.

Yet we go about our political life
acting and being exactly the opposite;
Republican and Democrat alike.
And still we have the arrogance
to stamp and print on our currency
"In God We Trust"

Friends, if "trust" is a realistic value,
it is time for some more hard questions:.

Have we had successful historical
models of confronting violence
and demanding justice
without using violence?
If the success of Gandhi in India,
the SCLC in America, Mandela and Tutu in South Africa worked,
why are we not training our military and police
to use these proven methods?

Who is in charge of the military here?
the generals with military intelligence
or we the people?

Why have all the leaders
of such systemic social change
in America and in history
all died violent
mysterious
deaths?

From the hill called Golgotha
to a motel balcony in Memphis

Humanity has shown how
deeply it is willing to
"Trust."

So, children, let's just start again
with the hard questions—
Do you believe in God?
Can we trust God?
Has God shown Her ways of trust?
Can trust bind us together?
Can we be one human family—
Living and working in peace?

Are you listening to these hard questions?
Then why are you responding
as if you are deaf in one ear
and can't hear out the other?

Club Med This is Not

Guantanamo,
Where we hold our prisoners of war
similar to Robben Island or Alcatraz
Prisoners to whom we have denied
any judicial and most human rights;
popularly called,
"Gitmo"

It was reported on the news this AM
that since we started bringing our
prisoners from far away Afghanistan,
Iraq, and who knows where else
Thirty-seven have attempted suicide;
Gitmo

That, in itself should say something
to the good Christian people of this
good Christian country about what
we have been doing to these human
beings such that we have driven
them over the edge of despair;
Gitmo

Today,
many Americans are willing to admit
that genocide of the Native Americans
who lived here before we stole all their land
moving the rest onto the worst land in the country
was a bad thing
but not Gitmo.

Today,
many Americans
are willing to admit
that the forced imprisonment
of Japanese Americans was racism
pure and simple and did nothing
to protect us during our
war with Japan. It was
a bad thing
but not Gitmo.
Today,
the enemy wears
a turban and has darker
skin than the Japanese but we
are treating him even worse,
if possible, than our
previous enemies;
Gitmo

Our good "Christian" President
and J. Edgar Ashcroft, head of our
"Justice Department" don't know the
first thing about Christianity or Justice.
Gitmo.

If they did, we would not have a
record of thirty-seven prisoners
attempting suicide, obviously
feeling they have no hope
whatsoever at the hands
of "good" Americans.
Gitmo

Robben Island or Guantanamo,
two more names of places where
the worst in human nature is
given free reign by
warrior kings.
Gitmo.

Sure doesn't make me feel
any pride in being an American,
given our new record of Christian
justice as demonstrated by
37 attempted suicides
in Guantanamo.

The Prerogatives of Power

Without a doubt, the most important breakthrough
in forensic science, since the discovery of the fingerprint
unique to each human being
is the discovery of DNA.

DNA is the quintessential lie detector leading to some sobering truths.
Using blood or other samples we now know contain DNA,
forensic scientists are able to identify, conclusively,
the DNA of a victim's attacker, even years after the event.

Then they can compare that finding with the DNA of
an accused and convicted person to see if they match.
Especially important if the prisoner
is awaiting execution.

Since its discovery, DNA evidence has freed over 130 prisoners
mistakenly convicted, 12 of whom were awaiting execution.
Sadly, others were discovered innocent
after they were executed.

This is cruel and unnecessary
punishment not worthy of a people
who claim to revere truth.

Now it has been revealed that prosecutors many times successfully block the testing of a condemned person's DNA until after execution. Then, after the convict is killed, they also oppose DNA testing after the fact.

One of the reasons given is cost.
Another is that victim's families
want and need cloture.
Life is cheaper
than truth.

Truth is given a back seat.—
we don't want to know.
our use of the death penalty is fatally flawed.
The system that asserts we can kill
others for the good of society
is itself now on trial.

We should be ashamed of past mistakes,
but this should not cause us to hide
the possibility of finding truth in
still others.

Especially when we have the means
to determine DNA truth.

The evidence is clear of the failure
of the criminal justice system
to prove guilt beyond a
reasonable doubt
I am amazed
that the Supreme Court
has not already denied the right
to take human life when means of
ascertaining truth have not been used.

A mistake here is irretrievable.
An apology will not suffice.

But such are the prerogatives of power,
To deny truth and truthful inquiry.
a pattern of willful deception
from the President on down.
Let the heads roll so that
survivors feel cloture
irrespective of an
innocent person
dying at our
hands.

Another oxymoron:
"Justice for all."

Let's Hear It for Spiders

The US Military, in its typical misuse of language,
has described Sadaam Hussein's final
hiding place as a "spider hole."

Spider man must be agonizing for where does
he rest when weary of saving the world?

I also would suggest that, had they a voice,
arachnids as a group would protest
to being compared to a tyrant
such as Sadaam Hussein.

But then our military while not noted for compassion,
is also inaccurate in just about everything
it does from abusing and killing
civilians, especially children,
to the use of language.

It's amazing to me they can walk and
chew gum at the same time.

Good Grief, Charlie Brown!

With thanks for the insight and research of
Dr. J. Shep Jeffries

This now famous comment
made by Lucy is symbolic of
her easy willingness to cast aside
the disappointments, sadness and grief
of those around her as of no consequence.

Yet as writers on grief show us,
grief is one of the most important and universal of human emotions.
It could serve as an emotion to unite the human family
if we could just remove our "Lucy mask,"
quit belittling this universal emotion
in others and within ourselves.

Part of what is wrong with our ongoing tragedy
in Iraq is our unwillingness to acknowledge
that different cultures grieve in different
ways. We have caused such
suffering that people who
normally would have

been gratified at
the capture of
Sadaam Hussein
now praise him which
is another way to say they
grieve at how he was removed
and what the war has done to them
by our hands.

This is not just a political response.
Grief counselors tell us that violent
and antisocial behaviors are
one of the red flags
that tell us when people
are captured in traumatic grief.
While clearly they need help,
one of the best things we could do
to help them would be to leave Iraq now.
Our military presence just makes the grief
worse and worse and worse.
One of the facts of warfare is war accelerates change,
change accelerates loss, and loss accelerates grief.
Seen clearly when parents, weeping,
caress the clothes of their child
lost in the rubble produced
by our bombs.

One thing is abundantly clear.
Continuing to be threatened with loss
will just increase and intensify grief.
Our presence, no matter how we
feel about our accomplishments
will intensify Iraqi feelings of
grief and outrage.

We can no longer act like Lucy
and pretend the grief we cause
is somehow excusable merely
because we captured Sadaam.

They know he was not
a direct threat to us.

In spite of all the political hoopla,
the world now knows there were
no weapons of mass
destruction.

I sometimes think
we learned nothing in Vietnam.
Two more wasted Bush wars with
unnecessary lies and suffering.

Oh, I know what all of those many who
still laud President Bush would say to me,
"Good grief, Charlie Brown!"

That doesn't cut it, Lucy
I am sorry, Iraq,
and I grieve
for your losses as for ours.

I Grieve This Christmas

I grieve because of this war.

I grieve that our President lied.
I grieve at the scorning of truth.
I grieve for the loss of community
slowly being built in the UN.
I grieve for our foreign service
officers who now have to face the
other countries' diplomats
knowing their President lied
and has been caught out.

I grieve for the unnecessary
body bags and grieve
with their families.

I grieve for the destruction of
Iraqi infrastructure and economy
and far too many civilians
and soldiers just to decapitate a statue,
get their tyrant and his oil.

I grieve at a Congress unwilling
to stand up to our tyrant on a
unilateral "crusade" in Iraq
(to use his own word)

I grieve mightily for
what we have done to our own
country and our own Constitution.
Holding people without benefit
of habeas corpus or even charges,
imprisonment without prompt and
speedy arraignment.
Not allowing benefit of counsel.
No benefit of trial by jury.

All of the guarantees that
made the Statue of Liberty
stand for something.

This war on terrorism looks to me
like a war on our rights won by
our ancestors struggling to get
out of European tyranny.

Now Bush and J. Edgar Ashcroft
show their true colors in
Guantanamo and
Abu Ghraib

If there is an orange alert of
imminent terrorist threat this
Christmas season it comes
not from without
but from within.

I grieve that we have no historical
memory and are creating a
"justice" system based on
injustice, wealth

and privilege
just like in the old country.

So much for inalienable rights
if you wear a turban and
speak Arabic and call
God Allah.

I suspect if those who signed our
Constitution and Bill of Rights
could see us now, there
would be a great
weeping and
wailing and
gnashing
of teeth.

Absolutism, Hubris and Prevarication

I shudder this first day of winter,
not from the cold but from the atmosphere—
a murky political atmosphere
consisting of **absolutism**,
which leads to unilateral war
against all moral advice.

Hubris which defines our nation as offensively contemptuous
of all who think or act different from us.

Presidential **prevarication** where we cannot trust
what he says about ourselves
or others.

Prevarication in the State of the Union address,
in the public relations gigs dressed in combat gear,
on carriers with lying banners,
or just in being a habitual liar.

Three dangerous habits even though
we have ancient wisdom
to guide us in such matters:

Lord Acton said it most clearly years ago,
"Power corrupts and absolute power corrupts absolutely."
A paradoxically absolute truth
now as when it was penned.

Reinhold Niebuhr regarded hubris as one of the classic flaws
of personal and political life.
The Bible warns against such
offensively contemptuous pride
as defined in ancient
and wise dictionaries.

"Thou shall not bear false witness."
One of the ten commandments with
no exemptions for a president or
any one else.
We are all subject to the tragedies of tornadoes,
hurricanes, earthquakes, floods, and wild fires
bringing devastation.
on the just and the unjust.
But we can prevent absolutism,
we can avoid hubris
and we can tell the truth.
Democracy, balancing powers,
humility in the face of others,
and basic honesty
can prevent human
caused tragedy

Wrapping tragic behavior in the flag,
declaring it as patriotic, doesn't cut it.
Blaming the CIA or the Arabs
doesn't cut it.
The ancient wisdom is still wisdom!

We best listen lest we go the way of all other empires.
Congress enabling such hubris in military tragedy
and then being an accomplice as
we are yet again lied to by the

emperor, Congress acting like
an enabler to a dry drunk.

Cleaning up after the tragedies of nature is bad enough.
But cleaning up after political tragedy
is intolerable, using our sullied
constitution to wipe up
the blood.

Oops!

In Bob Woodward's new book
President Bush briefs Saudi Arabia's Ambassador Bandar
and shows him the secret map of the impending Iraq invasion
before he shares this information with
the Secretary of State.

Is this a new way this President
is redefining the insiders and
outsiders of his cabinet?
or
Is this what is meant by thinking globally
and acting locally?
or
is this a part of Cheyney's Powell pummeling?
or
Is this just a new example of a Presidential "Oops"?

It's reassuring to know that for that advance look
Ambassador Bandar promised to
lower prices at the pump to
assist in Bush's reelection.
We're all waiting.

Now that's good reason to leave Powell out!
He doesn't have any power to manipulate
prices at the pump. So what good is he?
I wonder if the President misplaced
Colin Powell's phone number?
In their twelve minute meeting
he barely had enough time
to tell him to get on his
war uniform.

It's sad when you have to tell a general
when and how to dress.
Like God telling an apple tree
when to bloom.
I suspect Powell will rue the day he agreed
to serve as a peaceful diplomat for a
President who only wanted
a successful war.

20/20 Warfare

Northrop Grumman in another expensive full page ad in the Post
asserts that they can see clearly "*across an ever-widening range of threats . . .*
Only Northrop Grumman has the vision . . . to transfer the chaos of warfare into clarity." What this company proudly asserts is its ability to target anyone deemed the enemy in any global location allowing "***military planners shape the battle space . . . Deploy forces faster enabling total domination throughout: on the ground, at sea, in the air, space and cyberspace . . . . To ensure victory . . . .***" This is it, folks! In their own words, ***total domination***. last chillingly espoused by Adolph Hitler. While this company is certainly "***defining the future***" that does not give me any sense of increased security. If threats are ever-widening something is horribly wrong.
We must get at the root causes of these threats
which are and always have been:
hunger, poverty,
disease, economic
and environmental
devastation and
population explosion.
There are many causes
but ignored by a quest
for domination. Motivated
by greed and selfishly
protected by a military
infrastructure fed by
companies like
Northrop-Grumman
claiming they have
the vision of 20/20 warfare.
Tell that to the thousands of innocent Vietnamese
and Iraqi men,
women and children as well as some of our
own men and women who
lie in shallow graves today because of our brilliant 20/20
clear vision of warfare.
Is there not anyone anymore with a 20/20 vision for
peace on earth good will to all?

Now, Who Is Being Naive?

The whole time I was in university
pacifists (that's me) were accused of naivete.
We did not recognize the nature of evil
as demonstrated by Ho Chi Minh.
Our protesting of everything
from napalm to nuclear
was sneered at
as naive.

We lost that war.
Major players of that war like Robert McNamara
now admit that in retrospect everything
the protestors shouted at him
was correct. He was
the naive one.

It's chilling when our leaders today
in yet another war of American hegemony
say they don't understand how the Iraqis
and the world can regard us as an
occupying power, just
like in Vietnam.

Today, a conscience-struck Marine showed the world pictures
of Iraqi civilians we tortured and humiliated, and
the Post revealed we have spent hardly any
of the money authorized by Congress
for Iraqi reconstruction efforts,
while we have spent billions
bombing hell out of Fallujah.

I don't want to hear ever again
that naive, plaintive question,.
"Why do they hate us so?"

Now, who is being naive?

For Shame!

It makes no difference to the victims
or to their families or neighbors
nor to their nation
who is to blame.

The new picture of a naked Iraqi prisoner
clutching his prayer beads; his
bowed head framed by
prison bars mirrors
a scourged
Christ.

We should be ashamed as a nation
that we have spawned a military
and supportive politicians
that have produced
atrocities in our
name.

From the individual marine who held the leash
to the President and we who gave
him the money to pursue
his war.

We are all to blame.
We should be on our knees
asking forgiveness.

But unless we transform the way we do business
violence will continue to breed violence;
there will be no systemic solutions
only blame offered as a burnt offering
on the altar of Mars,
Our god of war.

Meanwhile I can only pray the suffering Christ
is mystically there to be with this man
as he prays for relief from
his suffering.

For shame!

The Best Government Going

I have been assured by loyal patriots
of both conservative and liberal
persuasions for years:

"We may not have a perfect government
but it's a damn sight better than
anything else out there."

It is a political reality that the Abu Ghraib scandal
would have toppled most governments
in the world. Why not ours?

With the media and Congress scurrying
to find people to blame (so we
don't have to look within)
we ignore the reality
our government
is to blame.

This is a systemic failure of a political culture
that relies on violence to produce
"intelligence" and solve
problems.

It is time to put our votes where our mouth is.
If we have the best government going,
it's past time to impeach them all,
bring the troops home, and
set the captives free.

Spain did it.
Will we?

Damage Control

In any crisis,
when the unexpected happens,
everyone scrambles to try to control the damage.

It is most unfortunate
when our leaders seem little concerned
about the abuse and mishandling of our prisoners
but most concerned about the pictures that told the world.

None of our leaders
want to admit that this is the way
we have treated prisoners of war for a very long time.
No one wants to honestly say like Pogo, "We have met
the enemy and
he is us."

Instead, we court-martial
the soldiers of whom we have the pictures
even though they said they were ordered to carry out the abuse
and some even released the pictures to the media because of
their guilt.

But in this truth shredding war damage control
consists in finding a scapegoat to sacrifice
so the public will believe the abuse was an aberration,
not the way we have been doing the business of warfare
for a very long time . .

The Motet

With thanks to Cheryl Oshman Blunt, Director

The motet and the madrigal forms of choral music evolved
at about the same time in history.
They were Renaissance choral music.
The madrigal was strictly secular, the motet had a sacred theme.

The motet had another difference that can speak to us today.
Sometimes the melody, usually carried by the tenors,
was sung in one language while the other parts
were sung in a different language.

In addition, the other parts were written to produce
an intended dissonance to the tenor's theme
who keep the melody suspended,
holding the dissonance until
stunningly resolved.

The "spiritual message" of the motet musical form seems
especially relevant today. We live in a very diverse world
with different languages and competing agendas..

Is it possible that God is singing the theme while the rest of us,
in our own languages attempt to assert an agenda of violence
that sounds a selfish dissonance?

In the motet, through the skill of the master composer
and expressed in a stunning resolution of the dissonance,
harmony is restored if we rediscover our oneness
in a music of the spheres.

The cacophony of school children, murdered and maimed in war,
is one more result of our prideful, competing agendas.
Man's wars will only find resolution if we humbly
seek God's restoration of harmony.
The hope is found in the reality
that any part can lead to
the resolution of
harmonic
peace.

To order additional copies of

Have your credit card ready and call:

1-877-421-READ (7323)

or please visit our web site at
www.pleasantword.com

Also available at:
www.amazon.com
and
www.barnesandnoble.com

Printed in the United States
24773LVS00002BA/121-189